Starting Your Own Childminding Business

More related titles

Book-keeping and Accounting for the Small Business
How to keep the books and maintain financial control over your business

'. . . compulsory reading for those starting a new business and for those already in the early stages.' Manager, National Westminster Bank (Midlands)

Preparing a Winning Business Plan
How to win the attention of investors and stakeholders

'This book will not only help you prepare a business plan but will also provide a basic understanding of how to start up a business.' *Working from Home*

The Small Business Start-up Workbook
A step-by-step book to starting the business you've dreamed of

'A comprehensive and very practical workbook offering a modern approach to self-employment. . . A *must have* for anyone thinking of setting up their own venture.' *Thames Valley News*

Work for Yourself and Reap the Rewards
How to master your destiny and be your own boss
'This book is written in a clear, concise and readable format. It's also very enjoyable.' CEO Business Enterprise Agency of South East Essex Ltd

howtobooks

Please send for a free copy of the latest catalogue:

How To Books
Spring Hill House, Spring Hill Road,
Begbroke, Oxford OX5 1RX, United Kingdom
info@howtobooks.co.uk
www.howtobooks.co.uk

Starting Your Own Childminding Business

Allison Lee

Published by How To Books Ltd
Spring Hill House, Spring Hill Road,
Begbroke, Oxford OX5 1RX, United Kingdom
Tel: (01865) 375794. Fax: (01865) 379162
info@howtobooks.co.uk
www.howtobooks.co.uk

First published 2006
Reprinted 2007

British Library Cataloguing in Publication Data.
A catalogue record for this book is available from the British Library.

ISBN: 978 1 84528 097 0

Cover design by Baseline Arts Ltd, Oxford
Produced for How To Books by Deer Park Productions, Tavistock
Typeset by PDQ Typesetting, Newcastle-under-Lyme, Staffs.
Printed and bound by Bell & Bain Ltd, Glasgow

NOTE: The material contained in this book is set out in good faith for general
guidance and no liability can be accepted for loss or expense incurred as a result of
relying in particular circumstances on statements made in the book. Laws and
regulations are complex and liable to change, and readers should check the current
position with the relevant authorities before making personal arrangements.

Contents

Acknowledgements   viii

Preface   ix

**1   What's Involved in Starting and Running a Childminding
      Business?**   1
      What it takes to be a good childminder   1
      Is there a need for the service in my area?   3
      Getting toys and equipment   5
      Outings and activities   7
      Financial planning and help   8

2   The Role of Ofsted and the National Standards   11
      The aims of the registration system   11
      Regulations   11
      Disqualifications   12
      The National Standards and what they mean   13
      Standard 1: Suitable person   13
      Standard 2: Organisation   14
      Standard 3: Care, learning and play   16
      Standard 4: Physical environment   17
      Standard 5: Equipment   18
      Standard 6: Safety   19
      Standard 7: Health   21
      Standard 8: Food and drink   24
      Standard 9: Equal opportunities   25
      Standard 10: Special needs   26
      Standard 11: Behaviour   27
      Standard 12: Working in partnership with parents and carers   28
      Standard 13: Child protection   29
      Standard 14: Documentation   30
      Caring for babies   31

3   The Registration Process   33
      Regulating childminders   33
      Who needs to register?   33
      Requirements for registration   34
      Applying to be registered   35

4   Setting up your Business   41
      Making your home safe for children   41
      Making your garden safe for children   48
      Choosing suitable equipment   51
      Travelling out and about   53
      A clean and healthy environment   55
      Accidents and emergencies   57

5	**Launching your Business**	60
	Creating the right image	60
	Deciding on the kind of service to provide	61
	Building a portfolio	63
	Working with another childminder or assistant	66
	Advertising	69
	Interviewing potential customers	72
	The first meeting	73
	Settling a child in	75
	Frequently asked questions	77

6	**Negotiating a Contract**	78
	Deciding how much to charge	78
	Charging for extras	80
	Agreed hours	82
	Settling in periods	83
	Retainer fees	83
	Deposits	85
	Childminder's holidays	85
	Parents' holidays	85
	Bank holidays	86
	Illness	87
	Responsibility for payment	88
	Playgroup, nursery, clubs	89
	Maternity leave	90
	Caring for children from the same family	91
	Signing the contract	92
	Reviewing the contract	93
	Terminating the contract	94

7	**Accounts and Bookkeeping**	95
	Your responsibilities	95
	Keeping on top of things	96
	How to keep your accounts	97
	Start-up costs	98
	Expenses	99
	Tax for the self employed	102
	Making a profit or a loss?	103
	What can I do if my business is making a loss?	105

8	**Everyday Running of your Childminding Business**	109
	Planning	109
	Daily routines	110
	Food and drink	116
	Keeping diaries	118
	How to write and maintain appropriate policies	119
	Parental permission	124
	Equipment checks	124
	Fire drills	126

Observations and assessments 126
Support groups and local community resources 128

9 **Providing Play and other Stimulating Activities** 132
What is play? 132
Different types of play 132
Categories of play 133

10 **Child Protection** 136
Types and signs of abuse 136
Allegations against childminders 141

11 **Causes for Complaint** 144
When things go wrong 144
Dealing with conflict 145
Difficult people and situations 148
Contract disputes 150
Areas of conflict 152

12 **Your Inspection** 155
The grading system 155
How to meet the standards successfully 156
How often will my setting be inspected? 160
Will I know my inspection date in advance? 160
What the inspection involves 161
What happens if the quality of care is considered inadequate 162
Being ready for the inspection 163
Questionnaire for parents 164
Self-evaluation 165

13 **Training** 166
Compulsory training 166
Certificate in Childminding Practice 167
National Vocational Qualifications for childminders 169
Quality Assurance 170
Childminding networks 170
Community childminding 171
Accredited childminders and early years education 171
Further training opportunities 171

14 **The National Childminding Association** 173
The role of the NCMA 173
The benefits of NCMA membership 174

Useful contacts 176

Index 178

Acknowledgements

Hand on heart I can honestly say that the best thing I have ever done in my life is to become a mother. My own children, Sam and David, have provided me with the inspiration for a career caring for children and I love every minute of it.

My husband, Mark, and my two boys have given me the love and support that has been needed for a demanding career in childminding. Despite the long hours, short holidays and stressful times that running a business can bring, they have always been there for me with encouragement and help and for this I am eternally grateful.

My mother, Cynthia, perhaps the most influential person in my life when it comes to childcare, has also been a source of inspiration and support. She has worked with me as an assistant over the years and shared the ups and downs that childminding has to offer.

I would also like to thank the following people and organisations for their contribution to this book:

Nikki Read and Giles Lewis of How To Books for giving me the opportunity to have my book published and help other people to realise their dream of setting up their own childminding business.

All the parents, carers and children I have had the privilege of working with over the years.

HMSO's Licensing Division for their kind permission to reproduce core material from Ofsted publications.

National Childminding Association.

All those who have contributed to the publishing of this book.

Preface

There are over 300,000 children in the UK who are currently being cared for by childminders, more than any other type of childcare. Statistics show that a large proportion of newly-qualified childminders fail in their business venture in the first year of becoming registered.

I believe that lack of support, after registration and during the first twelve months of starting a business, is a major factor in the contribution of such a high proportion of failed childminding businesses.

Demand for good quality childcare is high. Mothers are increasingly being encouraged to return to work after having children, and a high proportion of them look to childminders for a home-based setting in which their children can thrive.

I have been a childminder for over eleven years and during this time I have cared for more than fifty children ranging in age from 10 weeks to 11 years, from all walks of life. Some of the children I have cared for have been with me for years and others have been short-term placements. During my years as a childminder I have amassed a tremendous amount of knowledge and experience, much of which I would never have been able to gain by sitting in a classroom.

Starting Your Own Childminding Business is a book which is designed for you to discover whether or not a career in childminding is for you.

The book is aimed at helping you to find out what is involved in working from your home, with young children. It will help you to decide what level of commitment you are willing to make; whether you wish to work part time or full time, care for babies or older children and, ultimately, help you to decide if you have what it takes to be a successful childminder.

Do you have a dream of working from home? Are you under the illusion that working with children is all fun and play? If so then this book will, hopefully, draw your attention to some of the other aspects of childminding which are often overlooked.

My intention is not to put anyone off embarking on a career working with children – it is definitely the best decision I ever made from a career point of view, and I have never regretted becoming a childminder for a minute. However, it is important to start your career with your eyes open to the pitfalls. Despite the many 'highs' the job brings there are also a few 'lows' that you need to be prepared for, and be aware of how to deal with them.

Starting Your Own Childminding Business will help you answer the following questions:

- What is your ultimate goal?
- Do you want to work full or part time?
- What implications will working from home have on your family life?
- What facilities do you already have?
- What financial investment will you need to start your business?
- Can you raise the amount needed?
- Who will you aim your service at?
- How much will you charge?
- Will you need to advertise your business?
- What legal obligations do you have?
- Do you have the necessary skills and qualifications?
- If not, are you willing to train for them?
- Will you need to employ anyone?
- What factors are likely to hinder any progress you make?
- Are there any areas which you are particularly unsure of?

◆ If there are, do you know where to go for help and advice?

◆ Does your overall business strategy make sense?

◆ How long can you reasonably wait for your business to take off?

I hope this book will help you through the good times and the bad and you will finish up with a thriving, successful business.

I wish you every success with your venture!

1

What's Involved in Starting and Running a Childminding Business?

WHAT IT TAKES TO BE A GOOD CHILDMINDER

The most important reason for wanting to become a registered childminder has to be that you enjoy being with, and caring for, children. However, this is certainly not the only aspect you must be good at if you want your childminding business to flourish.

◆ TIP ◆

It goes without saying that your ultimate goal must be to provide the best possible care for the children and to keep them safe, and this is the very least parents will expect of you.

Working with parents

Parents looking for day care for their children are making one of the hardest decisions of their life. It is up to you to prove to them that they have made the right decision and to ensure that you will not let them down. They have trusted you with the most precious person in their life and they will come to depend on you, not only as a childminder, but as a friend and confidante. They may ask you for help and advice and it is very important, from the start, that you value the relationship you have with both the child and their parents, and build on this.

Childminding is very much a partnership and you must learn to work with the child's parents in order to provide the best care for the child so that they feel happy and secure.

Working alone

Planning and providing activities and resources are a very important and enjoyable part of being a childminder but there are also aspects of the job that you need to be aware of which are not as appealing and can, in fact, be quiet daunting.

Are you, for example, prepared for a life of mostly children for company with very little adult input? Childminding can be a lonely profession if you are stuck in the house all day with only very young children for company. It is possible to get around this by making use of drop in centres, mother and toddler groups etc, or you could consider working with another childminder, and we will look at this in more detail later in the book.

The effect on your family

Before embarking on a life as a childminder you must also ask yourself what the implications of the job will mean to the rest of your family. You may absolutely adore having children running around your home, wreaking havoc on your furnishings and painting the cat, but how does your husband feel when he is trying to get ready for work and a four year old is dressing up in his suit and carrying his briefcase? How does your 11 year old feel when a two year old has just scribbled all over the homework he has to hand in that morning? These are all aspects of childminding that you have to look at closely and questions that you have to ask yourself, and the rest of your family, and answer honestly.

◆ TIP ◆

It is vital to think through the implications that running a childminding business from home will have on the rest of your family.

Unless you are fortunate enough to work in a separate part of your house, which is completely cut off from your family space, then your childminding business *will* affect your home life. You must make sure, from the very outset, that everyone understands the implications that running a childminding business from your home will have.

It is perfectly possible of course to ensure the smooth running of your business so that it does not become a nuisance or annoyance to the rest of the family, but ground rules must be set and everyone must be organised sufficiently so that your business can run effectively.

Many parents choose a childminder over a nursery for flexibility. Some parents like the fact that their child is being cared for by one person in a home-based environment and it is very important therefore that you understand this, and your service must be available when it has been arranged. Of course no one can help being ill, but parents won't thank you for ringing them up, half an hour before they are due to drop their child off, to say that you have a headache and can't care for their child that day.

So to be a good childminder you need a number of qualities you must:

- enjoy being with and caring for children;
- be organised and use your time and space effectively;
- enjoy your own company or consider working with another adult;
- like people – be kind, considerate and helpful; and
- be flexible.

IS THERE A NEED FOR THE SERVICE IN MY AREA?

One of the biggest fears most people have when starting up their own business is not being sure whether there will be a market for their service. Of course there are no guarantees that your business will work, but there are certain things you can look at and research to get an idea of what you will need to provide, and what kind of competition you are up against.

You could have the most fantastic playroom ever built, with thousands of pounds worth of toys and equipment, but if you live in a quiet rural setting with no families nearby you are unlikely to succeed as a childminder. The service you are aiming to provide must work for the area you live in.

There are some important factors to consider when thinking about becoming a childminder.

Bus route
Not all people drive and if your premises are easily accessible by a main bus route it will be a more appealing option.

Schools
If you are a childminder living near a school you really should provide before and after school care.

Other childminders
If there are other childminders in the area, contact them about the service they provide and ask them for advice. Ask them if they are full and, if so, how many enquiries they have had recently.

New housing
Do you know of any plans to build new homes in your area? This is a good sign. If a new housing development is being considered in your area, providing family homes, you will have a whole new market to aim your services at.

Private nurseries
Don't be put off if there are private nurseries close by as parents looking for a childminder often have to consider all the options, including nurseries. It will, of course, mean that you will have more competition and although the service you provide will be very different, your fees may have to be even more competitive. Contact any local nurseries and ask for details of their services and fees so that you know what you are up against.

Local authority
Contact your local authority. They should be able to tell you whether there is a need for childminding services in your area. They should also

be able to let you know if there is a childminding co-ordinator for your area who will be able to inform you how many local childminders there are with current vacancies, and give you an idea how many parents have been seeking childcare services recently.

◆ TIP ◆

Do your homework! Make sure you know the kind of competition you are up against and aim to make your service better.

GETTING TOYS AND EQUIPMENT

Setting up a childminding business is just like setting up any kind of business in that you will need to purchase the basic equipment.

If you already have young children of your own you may well have most of the equipment already needed to start up your business. It may just be a case of ensuring that what you do have is appropriate, and in a good state of repair, and adding any other necessary items.

The basic equipment you will probably need if you are caring for babies and young children is:

- ◆ cot and new mattress - a travel cot would suffice;
- ◆ clean sheets and blankets;
- ◆ pushchair/double buggy;
- ◆ highchair;
- ◆ car seats;
- ◆ changing mat;
- ◆ potty/training seat;
- ◆ bibs, plastic plates, bowls, cups and cutlery;
- ◆ safety equipment
  - – harness for highchair and buggy
  - – reins
  - – fireguard
  - – stair gates
  - – smoke alarms

   – cupboard/window locks

   – drain covers (for outside areas).

Safety

You will be expected to prove that your home is safe and free from any potential hazards at the time of your inspection by Ofsted. It is a good idea to have all your safety equipment in place prior to this inspection, if possible. It may be worth bearing in mind that some parents will be happy to supply their own pushchairs and car seats and therefore it may not be necessary to purchase these beforehand but this is purely down to preference. If you do decide to use items supplied by the child's parents you must always ensure that they are safe and conform to the necessary standards.

Toys

The basic toys you will need if you are caring for babies and young children are:

◆ clean rattles and soft toys;
◆ games and puzzles;
◆ building bricks and construction toys;
◆ books with both paper and cardboard pages;
◆ paper, crayons, paints, collage materials;
◆ dressing-up clothes and role play accessories.

You can not be expected to have *every* toy or book to cover *every* child's situation or preference, but if you can provide the basic toys listed above you can then add to them as and when finances allow.

Some childminders may only wish to provide care for school aged children and obviously the toys and equipment needed for this age group will differ from that of a childminder providing care for babies and young children. You should think carefully about the kind of resources you will need.

◆ **TIP** ◆

It is worth mentioning in stores that you are a registered childminder. Some places, such as the Early Learning Centre, offer childminders a 10 per cent discount off their purchases. You will need to apply for a card and give details of your registration.

Sharing toys and equipment

You may wish to share your toys and equipment with other childminders and this is an excellent way of acquiring resources. Often some toys or equipment are only required for a short time and can be expensive to purchase. For example, if you are caring for a child who has broken a limb, you may wish to obtain a doll with a plaster cast or one that is in a wheelchair. A childminder you know may have one and it is always worth enquiring. Likewise, dressing-up clothes for doctors and nurses are a good way of introducing hospital visits to children.

In addition to buying or sharing toys with other childminders, you should also consider using toy libraries. Toy libraries lend toys to registered childminders for an agreed length of time, at a nominal charge. They can supply a large number of different toys suitable for a range of ages and abilities.

If you care for a child with additional needs you may find your local toy library particularly helpful as specially adapted toys can be very expensive to buy. Your local Children's Information Service (CIS) or Early Years Development and Childcare Partnership (EYDCP) will have details of toy libraries in your area.

It is also worth mentioning to your local library that you are a registered childminder as they will often allow childminders to borrow a greater number of books.

OUTINGS AND ACTIVITIES

In addition to providing toys and games you will need to think about, and plan, suitable outings to stimulate the children and provide fresh air and exercise.

It is often quite easy to provide interesting activities for older children for a couple of hours, before and after school, but have you thought of how you are going to fill a whole day if you are going to be caring for them during the school holidays? It is important that the children do not become bored and you should think of suitable outings as well as providing interesting activities.

It may be worthwhile investing in a selection of board games and perhaps, if funds allow, a computer with suitable learning programmes. Books and collage materials are always a sound investment, whatever the age of the child. In the summer months I have found it beneficial to involve the children in planning and preparing outdoor activities such as a cricket match or an obstacle course. Picnics and days in the park are also good ways of filling the school holidays when the weather permits.

◆ TIP ◆

Think about ways of providing spontaneous play. Children can have a lot of fun and enjoyment from events such as an impromptu walk following a downpour. Look out for rainbows and let the children wear wellingtons and splash in the puddles!

FINANCIAL PLANNING AND HELP

You will have initial expenses to get your business up and running, and it is important that you set yourself a budget and plan carefully how you are going to utilise it.

You will have to purchase basic toys and equipment, if you do not already have them, before you begin to work. Your Ofsted inspector will need to see that all your safety equipment is in place and meets the set standards before registration is granted.

In addition to toys and equipment you will need to purchase public liability insurance and pay for your registration and inspection fees.

It is possible to set up your business with limited funds providing you choose your equipment wisely and continue to add to your resources as and when you are in a position to do so. Toys and equipment suffer from a lot of rough handling and wear and tear is inevitable so it is vital that you check and replace toys and equipment regularly.

◆ TIP ◆

Set yourself a realistic budget and stick to it. Make a list of *necessary* items such as appropriate toys and equipment, registration fees, insurance, safety equipment etc and then draw up a *wish list* of items you would like to purchase when funds allow.

Start-up grants

Start-up grants for childminders are available in some areas of both England and Wales. These grants are aimed at helping new childminders with the cost of setting up their business and can be used to purchase toys, safety equipment, first aid training, insurance, registration and inspection fees and membership to the National Childminding Association.

The funds are distributed by Early Years Development and Childcare Partnerships and you should contact your local authority for details, together with any conditions that may apply. You will need to provide receipts for items purchased if you are hoping to pay for them through a start up grant.

Free milk

As a registered childminder you are entitled to claim for the cost of one third of a pint (189ml or 1/5th litre) of liquid milk per day for each child you care for under the age of five years. Infants under the age of one may instead receive dried baby milk made up to one third of a pint. The child must be in your care for more than two hours per day.

When you have become registered you should apply to the Welfare Food Reimbursement Unit (WFRU) at PO Box 31044, London, SW1V 2FD to request a form or telephone them on 0870 720 3063. You will need to supply your name and address together with your Ofsted registration number and the number of children, under the age of five years, you are registered to care for. You will be sent a form which must be completed with the number of children you have cared for each day, together with the cost of the milk you have purchased. The forms are for a four-month period and payment will be made to you accordingly.

◆ **TIP** ◆

It is important that you claim for your free milk entitlement. The amount can be quite substantial over a 12-month period and if you fail to claim your allowance it may cease to be available.

Sustainability grant

Early Years Development and Childcare Partnerships have, in the past, offered childminders in proven disadvantaged areas 'bridging grants' in order to help them out financially if they have had a vacancy for more than two weeks. This scheme has now been widened and EYDCPs now have funding which they can distribute in a number of ways including:

◆ continuing to provide 'bridging grants';
◆ producing leaflets promoting childminding;
◆ providing training to promote childminding businesses;
◆ funding support workers to help fill vacancies.

Each EYDCP has its own amount and type of funding and it is worthwhile contacting them if you have any vacancies to see if they can help financially.

Information about grants

Finally, it is worth looking at Business Link's website at www.businesslink.org or telephoning 0845 600 9006. Business Link offers advice to small businesses in England and has invaluable information regarding all aspects of running a business. As a childminder running a small business you may be able to benefit from a number of grants. Childminders working in Wales should contact Business Eye by visiting www.businesseye.org.uk or telephone 0845 796 9798. In Scotland, look at www.bgateway.com, and in Northern Ireland, www.investni.com/index/start.htm.

2

The Role of Ofsted
and the National Standards

THE AIMS OF THE REGISTRATION SYSTEM

The Children Act 2004 states that anyone who looks after other people's children in their own home must be registered with the Early Years Directorate of Ofsted in England or the Care Standards Inspectorate Registration in Wales.

It will be necessary, when applying for registration, for you to be able to prove to your local department that your home meets the legal requirements to provide a safe and secure environment for the children you intend to care for.

You will need to demonstrate that you are a suitable person to provide care for young children and that you take your responsibilities seriously.

The registration system is in place so that Ofsted can aim to:

♦ ensure that all childminders meet the National Standards;
♦ protect children and provide reassurance for parents/guardians;
♦ promote environments where children are safe and well cared for;
♦ ensure care contributes to development and learning;
♦ promote high quality childcare provision.

REGULATIONS

Ofsted regulates childminding in the following four ways:

Registration

This process covers checks on you and your premises together with any other adults who live or work on the premises where you intend to carry out your childminding service.

Inspection

Ofsted inspectors will carry out checks on your childminding service periodically. You will be issued with a report setting out their findings and any actions they feel you must take. This report must be made available to parents.

Investigation

An Ofsted Childcare Inspector may carry out an investigation into your childcare provision to check that you are meeting all the National Standards and requirements.

Enforcement

If necessary, Ofsted can take action against you if the National Standards and other requirements are not met.

◆ TIP ◆

It is a fineable offence to work as a childminder without being registered by Ofsted.

DISQUALIFICATIONS

Anyone wishing to become a registered childminder must meet the standards and conditions set out by Ofsted. There are certain factors that may disqualify you from becoming registered and if this is the case you will not be able to become a childminder.

Your registration may be disqualified if you or any person who lives or works with you has been:

- put on the Protection of Children Act list which considers a person unsuitable to work with children;

- convicted or charged with any offence against a child;

- convicted or charged with certain offences against an adult;

- listed on the Department for Education and Employment List 99 which considers a person not fit and proper to work with children.

A Department of Health guide to the Protection of Children Act 1999 is available on the government website www.doh.gov.uk/scg/childprotect.

THE NATIONAL STANDARDS AND WHAT THEY MEAN

There are 14 National Standards for Under Eights Day Care and Childminding. These standards cover all aspects of childcare in a range of settings. Inspectors from Ofsted (England) or CSIW (Wales) will use the criteria set out in these standards when considering your application to become a childminder. For information on what Standards apply in Scotland contact the Scottish Commission for the Regulation of Care, and for Northern Ireland, the NICMA (see Useful Contacts).

STANDARD ONE: SUITABLE PERSON

Adults providing day care, looking after children or having unsupervised access to them are suitable to do so.

For an adult to be deemed suitable to look after children, or have unsupervised access to them, they must first comply with all the conditions of registration. Conditions of registration include a vetting procedure where the information supplied is verified with the relevant sources. Police checks are also carried out to enable the inspector to determine whether the applicant is a suitable person to care for, or have regular contact with, children. To comply with Standard One you must be suitably qualified and agree to notify your regulatory body if you intend to employ an assistant.

Points for consideration

◆ Do you have the necessary training, qualifications and experience to make you a suitable person to provide day care for young children?

◆ Are you mentally and physically fit enough to care for young children?

◆ Are you able to make the correct decisions about the suitability of any assistants you may require to work with you?

◆ Are you free of any convictions which may make you a potential risk to young children or disqualify you from becoming a childminder?

◆ TIP ◆

You will need to be available to work regular long hours. If you or any member of your family suffers from a long-term illness you should seriously consider the impact this may have on your childminding business. You may be letting lots of families down if you need regular absences due to illness.

STANDARD TWO: ORGANISATION

The registered person meets the required adult:child ratios, ensures that training and qualification requirements are met, and organises space and resources to meet the children's needs effectively.

You should be able to provide resources and activities for children of a wide range of ages and abilities. You need to organise your day so that you are able to get to school, nursery and playgroup on time *every* time.

Numbers and ages

The maximum number and ages of children a childminder can *usually* care for at any one time are as follows:

◆ no more than six children under the age of eight years;
◆ no more than three of these six children may be under five years of age;
◆ no more than one of these children may be under 12 months old.

You may also provide care for children aged between eight and 14 years, however the number of children you agree to look after in this age category must not adversely affect the care provided for children under the age of eight years, and you must take into account the amount of space and resources you have available.

Any child aged four years who attends ten early years sessions per week will be allowed to be classed as a child over the age of five years for the purpose of the adult:child ratio.

Although the above numbers are the general rule, exceptions can be made in certain circumstances. For example, if you work with another childminder or employ an assistant the number of children you are registered for will increase. (If you employ a student on a training placement they are *not* included in the adult:child ratio.) Exceptions can also be made for siblings but it is very important that, should you wish to care for more children than stated on your registration certificate, you contact your regulatory body *prior* to commencing to care for the child in order to seek permission and to have your registration details amended to incorporate any changes they agree to make.

◆ TIP ◆

The adult:child ratios must include *all* the children on the premises and this means any children of your own and any others that you may be responsible for who are on the premises at the time of providing childcare.

If you already have three children of your own under the age of five years, you will not be allowed to care for any others between these ages. It is, however, worth considering caring for school-aged children before and after school and during school holidays. This will enable you to build up your business slowly and leave you free to offer childcare for younger children once your own children have grown.

Points for consideration
◆ Are you able to work with, and supervise the work of, an assistant, ensuring that they understand what you expect of them. Can you give clear and concise instructions?

◆ Are you organised in your daily routines?

◆ Do you utilise your space, time and resources efficiently?

◆ Are your training and qualifications up to date?

◆ Are you able to maintain the appropriate adult:child ratios?

◆ Can you keep accurate, up-to-date records of attendance, payments, sickness, medicine, administration etc?

STANDARD THREE: CARE, LEARNING AND PLAY

The registered person must meet children's individual needs and promote their welfare. They plan and provide activities and play opportunities to develop children's emotional, physical, social and intellectual capabilities.

As a childminder it will be your duty to encourage children to be independent and confident and you must try to build on their self-esteem. You must be available to listen to, and value, what a child has to say. You must be genuinely interested in the children you are caring for; talk to them, encourage them and help them to have high expectations of their own achievements and to believe in themselves.

As a registered childminder you must select and provide activities and experiences which are appropriate to the child's age and stage of development and which allow the child to explore and build on their natural curiosity. You must encourage children to develop social relationships, use their imagination and build on language and mathematical thinking.

Children should be encouraged to learn values and to respect other people and their belongings. They must be encouraged to learn about what is right and wrong.

It is important that you organise your resources so that they are readily available to the children and that you make the planning of first-hand experiences and spontaneous play a part of your daily routine. Whilst going about your everyday routines you should encourage the children in your care to ask questions and to use their imagination.

Early Learning Goals must be understood and implemented if you are part of an accredited childminding network and caring for funded three and four-year-old children.

◆ TIP ◆

As a childminder you need to be kind, considerate and patient. Children need to be able to approach you for love, assistance and reassurance.

Points for consideration

◆ Are you a kind, considerate and approachable person who can provide a warm, caring and loving environment for young children?

◆ Do you enjoy working with and encouraging children, offering assistance and praise when necessary?

◆ Are you able to manage children's behaviour effectively, setting fair and consistent boundaries?

◆ Do you have the necessary resources and experience to enable you to meet a broad range of care, learning and play needs in young children?

◆ Do you know when and how to listen to children, value what they have to say, encourage them to ask questions and respond to their interests?

STANDARD FOUR: PHYSICAL ENVIRONMENT

The premises are safe, secure and suitable for their purpose. They provide adequate space in an appropriate location, are welcoming to children and offer access to the necessary facilities for a range of activities which promote their development.

To meet the requirements of this standard, you must ensure that your premises are welcoming and friendly to both children and parents and are kept in a good clean state of repair and decoration. It is important that you ensure that you have all the necessary planning and building consents as stipulated by your local authority and that you ensure that the following minimum indoor space requirements are met:

♦ children under the age of two years require 3.5 square metres each;
♦ children aged two years require 2.5 square metres of space each;
♦ children aged 3–7 years require 2.3 square metres of space.

As a childminder you will be expected to provide suitable space for quiet activities and rest. Your premises must be well lit and ventilated with suitable washing and toilet facilities and you must have access to a telephone. An appropriate area must also be provided for the hygienic storage, preparation, cooking and serving of food.

If you are to provide an outdoor play area you must ensure that it is safe, secure and well maintained. If you do not have access to an outdoor play area then you will be expected to make arrangements for trips to the local parks or playground so that children in your care have regular fresh air and physical exercise.

♦ TIP ♦

Is there a local park or playground in easy walking distance from your home that you can take the children to visit regularly?

Points for consideration
♦ Are you able to provide a clean, safe, secure environment for children?
♦ Can you provide the necessary outdoor exercise?
♦ Are you able to plan and organise regular trips to your local park or playground if you do not have a suitable outdoor play area?
♦ Do you have appropriate washing, toilet and nappy changing facilities?
♦ Is your home adequately heated and ventilated?
♦ Can you provide the necessary space required for a number of children?
♦ Are you able to organise the space you have available effectively?

STANDARD FIVE: EQUIPMENT

Furniture, equipment and toys are provided which are appropriate for their purpose and help to create an accessible and stimulating environment. They are of suitable design and condition, well maintained and conform to safety standards.

All toys and equipment in your childcare setting, including any outdoor equipment, must be in a good state of repair and conform to BS EN safety standards or the Toys (Safety) Regulations (1995). You must ensure that all your toys and equipment are checked regularly in order that they remain in a good state of repair. Sufficient appropriate equipment must be provided for the number of children you are registered to care for so that the needs of all of the children can be met with regard to eating, sleeping and travelling.

As a childminder it is your responsibility to prove that you can provide sufficient, suitable toys and equipment for both indoor and outdoor play which will enable the children in your care to develop their emotional, intellectual, social, creative and physical skills. All equipment must be appropriate for the age and developmental needs of the children you are currently caring for.

Points for consideration

◆ Do you know how to carry out effective safety checks on your premises, toys and equipment and understand the necessity for regular checks?

◆ Do you understand how to choose toys and equipment, to suit a broad range of ages and abilities, which are interesting and stimulating as well as providing the necessary fun?

◆ Are you able to supply sufficient suitable toys and equipment for all the children you are providing care for?

STANDARD SIX: SAFETY

The registered person takes positive steps to promote safety within the setting and on outings and ensures proper precautions are taken to prevent accidents.

It is your duty to ensure that the children in your care are supervised at all times and are not subjected to any hazards whilst on your premises. You must make sure that your indoor and outdoor areas are secure and safe.

You need to pay careful attention to safety and hygiene issues at all times and make a detailed plan of the action you must take in the event of an emergency.

Outdoors

◆ You must ensure that **ponds, drains, pools** etc are inaccessible to children and that you closely supervise all water activities.

◆ Children should not be allowed access to **greenhouses, garages** or **sheds** unless these are made completely safe.

◆ You should ensure that your premises are kept free of any **hazardous plants or substances**.

◆ If children are to be taken on outings they must be **escorted safely** at all times.

◆ Any **vehicles** which you intend to use to transport children in your care must be properly maintained and conform to all legal requirements. You must have a valid driver's licence and the appropriate insurance. Children must be suitably restrained with the appropriate seatbelts or car seats.

◆ Written **parental permission** must be gained prior to outings and for transportation in a car.

Indoors

◆ All **gas, electric and other appliances** in your home conform to safety standards and do not pose a hazard to the children in your care.

◆ You must ensure that all **electrical sockets** which are accessible to children are fitted with socket covers.

◆ It is important that your premises are fitted with **smoke alarms** which conform to BS EN standards and that you check these regularly.

◆ A **fire blanket** which conforms to BS EN standards must be kept in the kitchen at all times.

- It is your responsibility to ensure that children are not exposed to any dangers and that they are **supervised** at all times.

- You must ensure that you have a suitable **emergency escape plan** which is regularly practised with the children in your care.

- You must comply with any recommendations made by your local **fire safety officer**.

- You must have valid **public liability insurance**.

Points for consideration

- Do you know how to ensure the safety of children both indoors and out?

- Are you confident when planning and arranging outings for children?

- Do your premises and equipment conform to all the necessary safety requirements?

- Are you able to ensure the safe arrival and collection of the children in your care? Are you aware of how to arrange suitable effective systems with parents?

- Do your premises have fitted working smoke alarms, a fire blanket and fire extinguisher? Are you aware of how to use this equipment and the need for regularly checking that it is in good working order?

STANDARD SEVEN: HEALTH

The registered person promotes the good health of children and takes positive steps to prevent the spread of infection and appropriate measures when they are ill.

Hygiene

As a childminder it is your duty to ensure that your premises and equipment are clean and that you and any assistant you may employ complies with good hygiene practices in order to prevent the spread of infection.

You must ensure that each child in your care has their own **towel**, flannel, bed linen, hairbrush and toothbrush (if this is appropriate). You should discuss with the parents who will provide them.

You should encourage the children in your care to practise good hygiene methods and to learn how to avoid spreading infections during your daily routine. Remember that you are setting the example for children to follow when it comes down to basic hygiene practice. You must teach the children to wash their hands after visiting the toilet, playing outdoors and blowing noses and before eating, and to cover their mouths when coughing and sneezing.

If you keep any domestic animals on your premises you must ensure that they do not pose a threat to the health of the children in your care and that they are safe from the risk of infection.

If you have a sandpit on your premises you must check that the sand is clean and, if left outdoors, that it is covered to protect it from contamination.

It is your responsibility to ensure that food is hygienically stored, prepared, cooked and served.

Medicines and first aid

You must not administer any medicine or treatments to a child unless the parent has provided it along with prior written permission. If you have been requested to administer medicine you must ensure that it is stored, according to its instructions, and in its original container and that it is clearly labelled and out of the reach of children. You must ensure that you understand what you are administering, and why.

You must keep written records of any medicines administered to children and ensure that the parent signs to acknowledge the administration. **If you care for a child who has a long-term medical condition** it is your duty to ensure that you fully understand the nature of the condition and obtain prior written permission to administer any medication.

You must hold a valid first aid certificate and keep a fully stocked first aid box on your premises at all times, the contents of which you must check regularly and replenish when necessary. It is advisable to purchase a travel first aid kit to take with you on outings.

When a placement starts you should get written permission to seek any emergency medical advice or treatment if necessary.

You must maintain signed records of any accidents in your care.

You must have a policy in place regarding sick children and this must be discussed and understood by the parents of the children in your care. This policy should include the exclusion of infectious children and your procedure for contacting parents or other designated adults should a child become ill whilst in your care.

You must practice a no-smoking policy whilst childminding and ensure that others on your premises refrain from smoking whilst you are carrying out your childminding duties.

Points for consideration

♦ Do you understand how to apply high standards of hygiene and why these standards are necessary?

♦ Are you aware of the ways in which infections are spread and how to prevent them?

♦ Are you aware of how to promote personal hygiene methods to children?

♦ Are you aware of the potential health and safety risks posed by animals and how to eliminate them?

♦ Do you know which medicines you are allowed to administer and follow the correct procedures when doing so?

♦ Do you know how to keep accurate records of all medicines administered to children?

◆ Do you understand the implications that smoking in the presence of a child has on their health, and can you ensure that no one is allowed to smoke on your premises whilst you are carrying out your childminding duties?

◆ **TIP** ◆

Your own personal hygiene must be beyond reproach. Children learn by example and you will need to teach them the rules of hygiene.

STANDARD EIGHT: FOOD AND DRINK

Children are provided with regular drinks and food in adequate quantities for their needs. Food and drink is properly prepared, nutritious and complies with dietary and religious requirements.

You must agree with parents which meals and snacks you are willing to provide and outline the kinds of food you will supply. Devising sample menus to show to parents is a good way of doing this.

As a childminder you must work closely with the parents to ensure that the child's dietary requirements are met and discuss any preferences or allergies. A written record should be kept of any preferences, allergies or special diets such as if a child is a vegetarian.

Fresh drinking water must be available to children at all times.

◆ **TIP** ◆

When planning meals you will need to take various factors into consideration such as cultural, religious and medical concerns. Always discuss these issues with the parents and *never* ignore what you have been asked to do.

Points for consideration
◆ Are you capable of planning and preparing healthy, nutritious food to cater for a variety of diets?

- Do you understand the importance of adhering to special dietary and religious requirements?

- Are you aware of the need to supply drinks to children regularly and when to increase their intake of fluids, for example on hot days and after physical exercise?

- Do you know where to obtain further information with regard to special diets or food preferences relating to religion, and is this information accessible to you?

STANDARD NINE: EQUAL OPPORTUNITIES

The registered person and staff actively promote equality of opportunity and anti-discriminatory practice for all children.

When thinking about the need to treat children 'equally' it is important that you do not fall into the trap of thinking that this means treating them 'all the same'. Childminders *do not* treat children all the same because children *are not* all the same!

You must ensure that you are familiar with the child's cultural background and that you liaise with the parents with regard to the appropriate care. The child's written records should contain the information supplied by the parent.

It is your duty as a childminder to treat all the children and adults for whom you are providing a service with equal concern, and ensure that you have regard for relevant anti-discriminatory good practice.

You must ensure that all the children in your care have equal access to the appropriate range of activities and facilities available.

Points for consideration
- Do you understand what is meant by 'equality of opportunity'?

- Do you have the confidence to challenge racist and discriminatory remarks?

◆ Do you have the ability to treat all children as individuals and with equal concern?

◆ Are you aware of appropriate resources to use in your setting which promote positive images to children?

◆ TIP ◆

It is essential for childminders to respect, tolerate, accept and learn from others. You must show awareness and sensitivity to people from all walks of life and with a variety of religions, customs and values.

STANDARD TEN: SPECIAL NEEDS

The registered person is aware that some children may have special needs and is proactive in ensuring that appropriate action can be taken when such a child is identified or admitted to the provision. Steps are taken to promote the welfare and development of the child within the setting in partnership with the parents and other relevant parties.

Childminders must ensure that children with special needs are provided with relevant resources to promote their welfare and development.

You must consult with the parents about the need for any special services or equipment which may be deemed necessary to provide for a child in your care.

If you identify a special need or disability relating to a child in your care you must share your observations with the child's parents and ensure that privacy policies are adhered to at all times.

◆ TIP ◆

Young children develop their values and attitudes from the adults around them. You must act as a role model for the children in your care. Always be prepared to challenge stereotypes.

Points for consideration

◆ Are your premises sufficiently equipped to provide suitable care for a child with special needs?

◆ Do you know how to keep appropriate records and how to share information beneficially with parents?

◆ Do you know how to include a child with special needs in your activities and daily routines, and why this is necessary?

STANDARD ELEVEN: BEHAVIOUR

Adults caring for children in the provision are able to manage a wide range of children's behaviour in a way which promotes their welfare and development.

It is advisable for childminders to adopt a behaviour policy which should be shared with the child's parents. Methods of managing children's behaviour should be discussed and agreed with the parents prior to commencement of the contract.

You must *never* smack or shake a child in your care nor use any other form of physical punishment. You need to be aware of, and able to implement, a variety of methods for dealing with a child's behaviour.

You must encourage good behaviour at all times and be consistent with your expectations concerning acceptable behaviour.

You should be aware of how to handle children's behaviour in a way that is appropriate to their age and development and therefore respect each child's individual level of understanding.

◆ TIP ◆

It is an offence for childminders to use, or threaten to use physical punishment against the children in their care.

Points for consideration

◆ Do you have a strategy for dealing with inappropriate behaviour and are you confident enough to carry this through?

- ◆ Do you understand the importance of dealing with inappropriate behaviour sensitively and know how to take into account a child's age and level of understanding?

- ◆ Do you recognise the need to discuss the methods you use to manage behaviour with the parents?

- ◆ What methods will you use to reward, value and encourage good behaviour?

STANDARD TWELVE: WORKING IN PARTNERSHIP WITH PARENTS AND CARERS

The registered person and staff work in partnership with parents to meet the needs of the children, both individually and as a group. Information is shared.

Written agreements must be kept with regard to the business arrangements expected by both yourself and the parents. Remember that parents are the most knowledgeable people in their children's lives. You must respect their wishes at all times and seek their views with regard to their child's preferences.

You must inform parents about your childminding routines and the child care practices you follow and you should be available to exchange information on a daily basis. Any complaints raised must be dealt with promptly and records of these must be maintained.

Written details must be kept and updated regularly with contact details for emergencies, doctor, health visitor etc.

If a child has been identified as a child in need (in accordance with the Children Act 2004) then you must, as a childminder, give the appropriate, accurate information to referring agencies. This is usually done with parental consent.

◆ TIP ◆

Never release a child from your care to anyone other than the individuals named by the parent. Consider introducing a 'password' system if a child in your care is frequently collected by adults other than the parents. Ensure that you *never* release a child unless the adult collecting knows the password, and has been approved by the parent.

Points for consideration

◆ Do you know how to write policies and implement them?

◆ Are you approachable?

◆ Do you understand the importance of confidentiality and know how to maintain this at all times?

◆ Do you realise the importance of parents in a child's life and the need to discuss the child's routines with them?

◆ Are you confident at keeping written records with up-to-date information about the child, parents etc?

◆ Do you know how to deal with, and record, complaints?

◆ TIP ◆

Parents know their children better than anyone else. *Never* offer advice unless you are asked for it or unless you know the parent very well, as it can be seen as interference or even criticism.

STANDARD THIRTEEN: CHILD PROTECTION

The registered person complies with local child protection procedures approved by the Area Child Protection Committee and ensures that all adults working and looking after children in the provision are able to put the procedures into practice.

As a childminder it is your duty to ensure that the protection of any child in your care is your first priority. You must be aware of, and be able to recognise, any possible signs of abuse or neglect and know who to contact in accordance with your local Area Child Protection Committee (ACPC).

You must record and report any concerns you may have according to the procedures. Ensure that the information is kept confidential and only given to the people who need to know.

◆ TIP ◆

Your first priority must *always* be the welfare of the child.

Points for consideration

◆ Are you knowledgeable in the different ways a child can be abused?

◆ Are you confident that you can spot any signs of abuse?

◆ Are you familiar with the procedures to follow if you suspect a child is being abused?

◆ Do you know how to handle any allegations of abuse made against you or anyone working with you?

STANDARD FOURTEEN: DOCUMENTATION

Records, policies and procedures which are required for the efficient and safe management of the provision, and to promote the welfare, care and learning of children are maintained. Records about individual children are shared with the child's parent.

You must make your records available for inspection by the early years' child care inspector, and you must retain records relating to children who have left your setting for a reasonable period of time.

You must inform the early years' child care inspector if any of the following changes to your provision have occurred:

◆ There have been any significant changes to your premises.

- There have been any allegations of abuse to a child whilst in your care.

- There have been any changes in the persons aged over 16 working or living in the household.

- There have been any other significant changes or events.

◆ TIP ◆

Do you have a suitable place in your house where you can safely store your documentation so that it is kept confidential and away from any prying eyes?

Points for consideration

- Are you organised and efficient when maintaining written records of the children in your care, and do you understand the need to regularly review and update these records?

- Are you aware of the confidential nature of your written records? Can you ensure that they are only seen by people concerned with each individual child's welfare?

- Have you considered how and where to store your records in order to ensure that they are not accessible to people whom they do not concern?

- Are you aware of which changes you need to notify Ofsted of and when permission needs to be sought?

CARING FOR BABIES

If you wish to care for babies and or children under the age of two years you will have to meet further criteria in addition to the 14 standards already looked at in this chapter.

You must be able to demonstrate that you have a sound understanding of the needs of babies and toddlers and that you understand the need to spend time interacting with them at frequent intervals throughout the day. You must be knowledgeable about the toys and equipment suitable for the child's age and development and ensure that they are not given access to any toys or other articles which may cause them harm.

You must respect the sleeping, feeding and nappy changing routines of each individual child and provide adequate sterilisation for feeding bottles and utensils as well as the safe preparation and serving of baby food.

Looking after babies, although extremely rewarding, can also be very demanding. You need to be sure that you have the time and energy to devote to caring for babies and that you can provide adequate care for them around your existing daily routine. Remember babies do not fit around your lifestyle – you must fit around theirs!

3

The Registration Process

REGULATING CHILDMINDERS

Ofsted regulates childminders using the following four methods:

- registration;
- inspection;
- investigation;
- enforcement.

By using the above methods Ofsted aims to:

- protect children;
- enforce the National Standards;
- promote high quality childcare;
- ensure that children are well cared for in safe environments which enable them to take part in learning activities which contribute to their development;
- help to reassure parents.

WHO NEEDS TO REGISTER?

As a childminder you need to be registered by Ofsted if you look after one or more children under eight years of age, for more than a total of two hours per day, on domestic premises, for any kind of reward. 'Reward' in this case does not necessarily mean money. Accepting presents or payment 'in kind' is also viewed as 'reward'. It is an offence to act as a childminder without being registered and if discovered you may be liable to a fine.

There are, however, people who can care for children without being registered as a childminder, and they fall into the following categories:

♦ If you are the parent, or relative of the child you are looking after, or if you have parental responsibility for the child.
♦ If you are a local authority foster parent in relation to the child.
♦ If you have fostered the child privately.
♦ If you only care for the child between the hours of 6pm and 2am.
♦ If you look after the child wholly or mainly in the child's own home.
♦ If you care for children from two separate families wholly or mainly in either or both of the children's own homes.

♦ TIP ♦

Looking after children for reward does not have to mean you are receiving financial gain. It is an offence to care for someone's children whilst not registered even if the payment is a bunch of flowers or a box of chocolates!

REQUIREMENTS FOR REGISTRATION

You have to prove that you can meet certain requirements prior to Ofsted agreeing to grant registration. Ofsted will be looking for the ways in which you can demonstrate that:

♦ You agree to comply with the National Standards (as set out in Chapter 2 of this book).

♦ You agree to comply with any regulations and conditions which your regulatory body may feel necessary to impose on you.

♦ You are a suitable person to look after children under the age of eight years and that any other person working with you is also suitable.

♦ Every person living or employed on the premises is suitable to be in regular contact with children under the age of eight years.

♦ That the premises where you intend to carry out your childminding business are suitable for the purpose of caring for children under the age of eight years.

In addition to complying with the National Standards, regulations and conditions imposed on your registration, you must also ensure that you notify Ofsted of any:

- alterations to your premises or childcare provision;
- changes to any assistants, employees or family circumstances;
- circumstances which may affect the welfare of any children in your care.

There are some factors that would automatically prevent you from becoming a registered childminder and these are looked at in Chapter 2.

APPLYING TO BE REGISTERED

The chart below shows the basic steps of the application process which you have to go through for a decision to be made as to whether you may become a registered childminder.

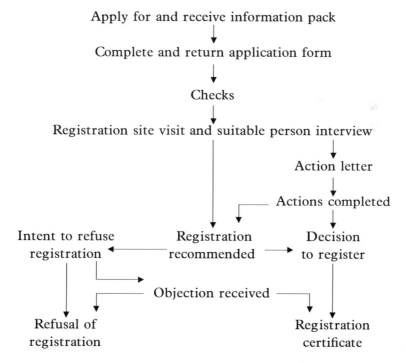

◆ TIP ◆

> It is important to remember that Ofsted are looking to register you. They are not trying to find reasons *not* to register you. They are checking your suitability to work as a childminder and to provide for the children. They can offer help and advice on any changes they feel need to be made in order for your registration to go through.

We will now look at the steps in more detail so that you can be aware of what is involved during your application process and what will be required from you.

Information and application pack issued and returned and checks

To obtain an information pack you should contact your local authority. They will also supply you with details of pre-registration briefing sessions and information about registration courses and training. You should also request copies of the National Standards and Guidance to the Standards when requesting your application pack and read these carefully before applying to become registered.

The application pack contains general information regarding the childminding registration process together with the following four forms:

1. **CM1**: This form requests information about you and the premises where you intend to operate your childminding business from.

2. **CM2**: This form asks for a declaration about criminal records and matters of suitability to care for young children and also asks for your consent for Ofsted to make checks with certain other professionals including:
   - social services (child protection register, social service records)
   - your GP
   - police officers/Criminal Records Bureau
   - Protection of Children's Act list
   - Department for Education and Skills List 99

– referees

– previous employers

– health visitor

– the registered homes list.

3. **Health declaration form**.

4. **Police check form**: As you are requesting to register to care for young children you will need to apply for an Enhanced Criminal Records Disclosure from the Criminal Records Bureau (CRB) for yourself and every person over the age of 16 who will be living or working on the premises.

The results of all these checks will be taken into account by Ofsted when assessing your suitability and processing your application to become a registered childminder. It is important that you complete the forms as directed and return them with the appropriate *original* documents requested to ensure that your application is processed without delay.

Registration site visit and suitable person interview
There are three main reasons for a site visit and suitable person interview and these are as follows:

1. To enable the inspector to ensure that you are qualified and prepared to begin the task of caring for children in your home.

2. To enable the inspector to satisfy themselves that your premises are safe and suitable for children to attend.

3. To decide how many children you may be registered for, taking into account the space and resources you have available.

Many childminders feel apprehensive about their suitable person interview and this is understandable. It is important to remember, however, that the inspector is not working *against* you. Their aim is to find out whether you have the necessary aptitude to work with young children and, if they feel that improvements can be made, then these will be addressed. The inspector is not looking for faults in order to refuse your registration, they are satisfying themselves that you meet the necessary criteria and will offer help and advice where necessary.

◆ TIP ◆

The Ofsted Inspector is *not* your enemy. They are looking at your suitability to work with, and provide for, the needs of children.

Preparing for site visit and interview

You can prepare yourself for your registration site visit and suitable person interview by studying the Guidance to the National Standards, which you will have received with your application pack. It is important that you are familiar with the National Standards at this stage as the inspector will discuss these with you at your interview. You will be expected to show how you will meet the Standards in your work and demonstrate your knowledge of identifying and minimising any possible risks to health and safety.

Prior to your registration site visit, which will be arranged by the inspector at a mutually convenient time, you must ensure that you are in possession of all the relevant documentation such as proof of any training and qualifications. At this stage Ofsted will usually have carried out all the necessary checks and they will already have received the appropriate references.

◆ TIP ◆

Make sure that you have read the Guidance to the National Standards and that you are familiar with the necessary criteria. The Ofsted inspector will discuss these with you at your suitable person interview.

The inspector will use the information gathered at your interview, together with the checks already made, to assess whether or not you are considered a suitable person to be registered and ready to begin working as a childminder.

After conducting your interview and prior to leaving your setting, it is usual for the inspector to give you oral feedback on the outcome of the visit in order that you are clear about anything they may feel needs to be done prior to Ofsted granting your registration. There may be conditions imposed on you – something as simple as not allowing children access to certain outside areas if they feel there is a hazard, a pond or greenhouse, for example. *Now* is the time to ask any questions and discuss any actions or conditions.

Action letter

In some cases, an inspector may feel that changes need to be made to your premises in order to comply with the National Standards. Any changes deemed necessary will have been passed on to you verbally during your suitable person interview and the action letter will put these requirements in writing, detailing an appropriate timescale for any work to be carried out.

> ◆ TIP ◆
>
> Sometimes the 'conditions imposed by Ofsted' are very simple such as restricting access to any hazardous areas. The conditions are part of your registration and you *must* agree to them for registration to take place.

Decision to register

Following a satisfactory site visit and suitable person interview, Ofsted will notify you in writing of their decision to register you as a childminder. Their decision may contain certain conditions which you must agree to comply with, and these will be outlined in the letter. At this stage you will be required to pay the registration fee of £14 and provide written acceptance of any conditions imposed on your recommendation for registration. Ofsted does not normally grant registration until this fee is paid and a delay in sending the fee will mean a delay in issuing your registration certificate.

Registration certificate

The certificate will contain your name, address and any conditions imposed with regard to your registration. This certificate is your proof of registration and must be shown to prospective parents seeking childcare. It is a good idea to display your registration certificate in your childminding setting. If you decide to stop being a registered childminder you will be asked to return your certificate to Ofsted.

◆ TIP ◆

Your registration certificate will not be issued until Ofsted are in receipt of your registration fee. You are advised to pay this fee promptly!

Intent to refuse registration, objection and refusal

A notice of intention to refuse your application will be issued by Ofsted if they feel you do not meet all the requirements of registration. This notice will include the reasons for your refusal.

If you wish to object you can do this by notifying them, in writing, within 14 days of receipt of the letter. Ofsted will assume that you do not wish to object to their decision if they have not heard from you within the 14-day period, and will then issue a letter confirming the refusal in writing. At this stage your right to appeal would have to go to an independent tribunal.

4

Setting Up Your Business

MAKING YOUR HOME SAFE FOR CHILDREN

In order to become a successful childminder it is paramount that you take your responsibilities seriously at all times. You must know what constitutes danger, how to avoid it and how to reduce the risk of accidents. Obviously accidents can, and do, happen – even to the most diligent of childminders – and so you must also know how to deal with accidents when necessary. The children in your care must be safe at *all* times; whether they are in your home, garden or on an outing *you* are responsible for their safety.

The Royal Society for the Prevention of Accidents (RoSPA) reports some rather alarming findings with regards to accidents in the home:

- The most *serious* accidents occur in the kitchen and on the stairs.

- Accidents occur most *often* in the living and dining room areas.

- Children up to the age of four are most at risk from an accident.

- Most accidents happen from late afternoon to early evening, mainly during school holidays and in the summer months.

- Boys are more likely to have an accident than girls.

- Each year nearly 68,000 children have an accident in the kitchen; 66 per cent of these accidents involve children under the age of four.

It is therefore easy to see that young children must be supervised at all times and that any potential dangers are assessed and removed wherever possible. It is not my intention to frighten potential childminders by giving these statistics, nor am I suggesting that you refuse to care for boys aged from birth to four years or that you ban all children in your care from entering the kitchen, living room or dining room! I am simply trying to point out that children are inquisitive, they love to explore – quite often in places they are not meant to be – and they have absolutely no understanding of danger.

Your responsibility

As a childminder the responsibility for the safety of the children in your care lies entirely with you. You will have to prove to a visiting Ofsted inspector, prior to becoming a registered childminder, that your home is safe. It is not sufficient to recognise the dangers and address them when time or finances are available. Unlike budgeting for new toys, as and when money allows, you will be expected to pay for any safety equipment or necessary alterations before registration is granted and you will have to meet all the necessary safety requirements. It is then up to you to ensure that your premises *stay* safe.

In order to help you to assess your home and decide which safety measures you need to address, we are going to look at each room separately. First, it is a good idea to think about your own family and ask yourself a few simple questions.

1. Has anyone in your family had an accident in the home recently?
2. If so, where did the accident happen?
3. Could the accident have been avoided?
4. Was anyone hurt?
5. Were they hurt seriously?
6. Did they need to go to hospital for treatment?
7. How did you handle the situation?

Do the answers you have given tell you anything about the safety measures already in place in your home? Ask yourself honestly whether your home is safe for young children.

> ◆ **TIP** ◆
>
> Safety should not just be thought of in terms of materials and equipment. Safe working practice is just as important as the tools you use.

Assessing the risks

Another very good way of assessing risks to young children is to see potential dangers through *their* eyes. So get down on your knees, crawl around your living room and look at the space from a child's level. Did you realise that the sharp edges on your coffee table are at exactly the same height as a toddler's eyes, ready to cause a serious accident should they trip and fall? Is the flex of your table lamp in just the right place to cause the toddler to trip and fall onto the coffee table?

It is, of course, impossible to remove every aspect of danger from your home, otherwise you would be caring for children in a completely empty room with padded walls and floors. The odd bump and bruise is part of growing up; it is the serious accidents that we are trying to avoid at all costs.

The kitchen

The dangers in this room are both obvious and numerous. Every house will of course be different but you should consider the following safety aspects in your kitchen.

- ◆ **Ovens**: Keep oven doors shut at all times and ensure that children cannot touch the oven door when it is hot.

- ◆ **Hobs**: Make sure that children cannot reach the hob and that all pan handles are turned away from the edge of the cooker or hob.

- ◆ **Fridge/freezers**: Make sure that the doors to fridges and freezers are securely shut at all times.

- ◆ **Washing machines**: Ensure that doors to washing machines are shut at all times and if you have a child lock, use it.

- ◆ **Tumble driers**: Ensure that the doors are shut at all times.

◆ **Hot objects**: Check that no hot objects, including cups of tea/coffee, pans, etc, are left near the edge of kitchen units, work surfaces or tables.

◆ **Cleaning materials**: All cleaning materials should be kept either in a locked cupboard or out of the reach of children. Cleaning fluids should always be stored in their original containers.

◆ **Medicine**: All medicine should be stored in a locked cupboard out of the reach of children. If medicine has to be stored in a fridge, consider fitting a fridge lock.

◆ **Alcohol**: Alcohol must be stored out of the reach of children or in a locked cupboard.

◆ **Plastic bags**: These should be stored out of the sight and reach of children.

◆ **Knives**: All knives and sharp objects should be stored out of the reach of children, preferably in a secure cupboard, and never left on kitchen worktops.

◆ **Kettles**: Kettles should be pushed to the back of the work surface. Ensure that flexes are out of reach and not dangling near the edge of work surfaces or kitchen units.

◆ **Electrical equipment**: All microwaves, irons, toasters etc should be stored out of the reach of children and the flexes must not be accessible to children.

Living room/play room

◆ **Ornaments**: Do not place ornaments or other small decorative objects in the reach of young children. Apart from the obvious risk of breakages they can be swallowed or inserted into ears or noses.

◆ **Floor space**: Ensure that the floor area is as clutter free as possible. Try not to allow children to get too many toys out at once and aim to put something away every time you get anything else out in order to minimise the risk of tripping over objects or standing on them and slipping.

- **Hot drinks**: Never leave hot drinks on coffee tables – always place these well out of the reach of children. Remember, even a cup of tea or coffee that has been left standing for ten minutes can seriously scald, and scar a child if spilt on them.

- **Storage**: Think carefully about where you are going to store the children's toys. Choose your storage sensibly so that toys are easily accessible and children do not have to climb or reach high to retrieve objects. If you opt for shelves make sure that they are securely fastened to the walls and cannot fall on to a child.

- **Plants**: If you have houseplants ensure that they aren't poisonous (see list of poisonous plants at the end of this chapter), and that they are placed well out of the reach of children.

- **Cigarettes**: It is a requirement of registration that childminders do not smoke whilst working with the children in their care. However, if you are a smoker, you will have cigarettes and lighters or matches in your home. You must keep these out of the sight and reach of children at all times.

- **Fires**: Fires are one of the most dangerous appliances in your home. Not only can they burn an inquisitive child, they can ignite toys, clothing, paper, books etc if they are close by. It is essential that a firmly fixed fireguard is in place around the *whole* of the fireplace at all times. Your home must be fitted with smoke alarms and you must check these regularly. It is also important that you have a fire blanket and a fire extinguisher in your home and that you know how and when to use them.

- **TVs, videos, DVDs etc**: Always ensure that the flexes to all electrical equipment such as televisions, videos, DVDs, computers, CD players are not left trailing and that they are out of the reach of children. In the case of video recorders, consider fitting a guard to prevent a child from inserting objects into the recorder. Apart from prolonging the life span of your video recorder, it will prevent small fingers from becoming trapped.

◆ **Toys**: Check toys and equipment regularly for broken pieces, missing parts or sharp edges and ensure that items are either repaired or replaced as necessary.

◆ TIP ◆

Children often enjoy playing in places they are not meant to be in and with objects they are not meant to have. The most effective method of preventing an accident is to ensure that the children are in your sight and sound at *all* times.

Dining room

It is very important that children are never left unattended whilst eating or drinking. They must be supervised at all times when there is hot food and drink around, and you should ensure that children are seated and not allowed to wander around when they are eating and drinking.

◆ **Tables**: Objects on tables should not be near the edge. Make sure that tablecloths do not hang over making it possible for small children to pull objects onto themselves.

◆ **Seating**: Ensure that all children, whatever their size, can sit safely and comfortably at the table using either highchairs or booster seats fitted with appropriate restraints.

◆ **Crockery/cutlery**: Children should be supplied with crockery and cutlery appropriate to their age and stage of development. Teach children the correct way to use cutlery and do not allow them to play with knives and forks.

◆ **Bottles**: Never leave a baby propped up with a feeding bottle.

Sleeping areas

◆ **Pillows**: Never use pillows for children under the age of 18 months.

◆ **Beds/cots**: Beds and cots, together with their mattresses must conform to legal requirements. Clean bed linen must be supplied for each child.

◆ **Supervision**: Children must be supervised at all times, even when they are asleep.

Bathroom and toilet
- **Water**: Hot water, which should be available for washing at all times, should not exceed 54°C. If running a bath or sink of water for washing always turn on the cold tap first and test the water temperature before allowing a child to use it.

- **Medicines**: Medicines should be stored in a locked cabinet out of the reach of children.

- **Cleaning materials**: All cleaning materials, air fresheners and disinfectants should be stored in their original packaging and out of the reach of children.

- **Supervision**: Young children should be supervised when using the bathroom or toilet. It is important, however, that you are conscious of the needs and ages of the children and respect their privacy.

Hall and stairs
- **Gates**: Gates should be fitted at both the top and bottom of the stairs. Make sure that all safety gates conform to BS 4125 standards and that they are firmly fixed in place. Choose gates that open rather than fixed gates which you have to climb over as these can be very dangerous, particularly at the top of a flight of stairs.

- **Space**: Ensure that stairs are free of any clutter at all times. Never allow the children to play on the stairs or leave any toys or belongings on them.

- **Carpets**: Replace any frayed, worn or loose carpets.

- **Banisters**: Make sure that your banisters and balustrades are strong and that there are no opportunities for children to climb onto them.

- **Windows**: Never place objects or items of furniture which a child can climb on under windows.

- **Lighting**: Ensure that your hall and stairs are well lit at all times.

Adequate supervision
You have both a moral and legal obligation to ensure that the children in

your care are safe at all times. It is essential that you are aware of the potential dangers in your home and that you carry out a risk assessment to minimise any accidents to the children you are caring for. You must look at your home critically and replace or remove any potential hazards.

However, even after diligently checking your home and conforming to all the necessary regulations it is still not possible to guarantee that an accident will not happen. The most important thing to remember, and the one thing that will *always* reduce the risk of an accident, is to ensure that you adequately supervise the children in your care at all times.

MAKING YOUR GARDEN SAFE FOR CHILDREN

Once again, the most obvious way to ensure that children are safe whilst playing outside is have them in your sight and sound at all times. Young children should not be allowed to play outdoors alone. In addition, there are other aspects which must be considered if you are to allow children to use your garden.

If your garden has a long list of potential hazards which may be expensive or impractical to alter, such as a garden pond, then it may be worth considering fencing off part of your garden to use solely as a childminding playground. This will of course depend largely on the size of your outdoor space, but it is something worth considering if allowing children the free run of your garden proves difficult from a safety point of view.

Safety issues in your garden

◆ **Access:** Ensure that the area the children will have access to is fenced off. Make sure they can't gain access to ponds or water butts.

◆ **Drains:** All outside drains must be fitted with suitable covers.

◆ **Rubbish:** Children must not have access to dustbins, compost heaps or other waste disposal sites.

♦ **Play equipment**: Make sure that all large play equipment such as swings, slides, etc is checked regularly for wear and tear, and that any loose or missing parts are repaired or replaced immediately. Large play equipment must be securely fastened to the ground to avoid tipping and suitable mats or wood chippings used underneath to ensure that children are not exposed to hard surfaces if they fall.

♦ **Washing lines**: Washing lines must not be strung across the children's play area. If rotary washing lines are used they must be removed or adequately covered to prevent children from becoming entangled in them.

♦ **Play area**: Your outdoor play area must be free from any dangerous or poisonous plants or trees (see list below).

♦ **Pets**: Never allow any pets to be exercised in the area designated for the children to play in.

♦ **Garden equipment**: Make sure that any garden equipment and tools are safely locked away out of the reach of children.

♦ **Greenhouses**: These must be fitted with protective glass film, fenced off or removed from the play area.

♦ **Ride-on toys**: Ensure that all ride-on toys such as bicycles are in good condition and well maintained.

♦ TIP ♦

There is a fine balance between taking reasonable and sensible care of children, and allowing them some risk taking when meeting new challenges and experiences. Never encourage a child to attempt something they are not happy to do, and always be on hand to offer help and assistance when necessary.

Poisonous plants and trees

The following is a list of some of the more common plants and trees which should be avoided when considering what is suitable for a garden to be used for young children. If your garden has any of these plants or trees you must remove them, or fence them off to restrict access by children:

- laburnum
- leopard lily
- wild arum
- oleander
- winter cherry
- poinsettia
- deadly nightshade
- hyacinth
- thorn apple
- woody nightshade
- yew
- hemlock
- poison primrose
- daffodil bulbs
- rhubarb leaves

- monkshood
- angels trumpets
- autumn crocus
- lily of the valley
- daphne
- foxglove
- spurge
- glory lily
- ivy
- hellebore
- lantana
- the poisonous primula
- castor oil plant
- rue

Some of the symptoms of poisoning from the plants listed above include:

- diarrhoea
- dizziness
- vomiting
- drowsiness
- blistering of the skin
- itchy rashes.

If a child in your care experiences any of these symptoms after coming into contact with poisonous plants you should consult a doctor immediately.

In addition to poisonous plants and trees which can cause harm to children, it is also advisable to avoid planting anything with unusual or colourful berries which may prove a temptation to young children. Nettles and thistles should also be removed to prevent stings and scratches.

CHOOSING SUITABLE EQUIPMENT

Toys

It is important when purchasing new toys and equipment that you ensure that they conform to the necessary standards. It is good practice to look for one of the symbols or logos associated with British Safety Standards whenever you are looking at new toys or equipment. Some items will have a BS number to show that they conform to certain safety standards whilst others will show the letters CE, the kite or the lion mark.

Despite strict regulations in this country for the manufacture of toys and equipment it is still possible to buy cheap imitations which are both illegal and unsafe and you must be careful to avoid these at all costs. Take particular care if you are purchasing toys from car boot sales, jumble sales etc, and always look for the necessary safety symbols.

Baby walkers

I would never advise anyone to purchase a baby walker. They can be a very dangerous piece of equipment and evidence has shown that baby walkers can actually hinder a child's development. Childminders are discouraged from using them.

High chairs

High chairs should be sturdy and placed on a flat surface so that they do not wobble. It is not advisable for childminders to use table-mounted high chairs as they are not considered sufficiently stable. Children should never be left in a high chair unsupervised, and high chairs must always be fitted with suitable harnesses which should be adjusted to fit the size of each child using them.

Baby seats

Baby seats should always be placed on a flat sturdy surface when not in the car and never on a table or work surface. Harnesses must be fitted and adjusted to suit the individual child.

Safety gates

They are a vital part of your safety equipment. Safety gates should be securely fitted with adequate childproof fastenings. Although they are essential for stairs they are equally useful to prevent children from gaining access to other rooms which may pose dangers, such as the kitchen.

Locks

It is advisable to use window locks in the rooms which the children in your care will have access to.

Prams and buggies

It is essential that you check and regularly maintain your prams and buggies. Check for wear and tear and broken pieces and repair or replace whenever necessary. Always use a suitable harness which can be adjusted to suit the child using it. As with car seats, some parents may provide a pram or buggy for you to use. It is just as important to check these for wear and tear as it is to check your own equipment and if you feel that the item is a danger to the child you must notify the parent immediately and refrain from using it.

Cots and beds

Mattresses should fit the cot or bed properly and conform to safety standards. You should not use pillows for children under the age of 18 months and young children should not be put into a top bunk. Travel cots are sufficient for the purpose of childminding, but if you do opt to purchase a cot with sides that slide down it is essential that they have secure childproof fastenings. Before purchasing bed guards consider how tempting these rails are for children who see them as potential climbing frames!

Potties and toilet seats

It is possible to purchase toilet seats which are designed to fit over a standard adult seat. If you choose to buy one of these it is important that the seat fits firmly and that you supply a secure step for the child to reach the seat without having to climb or pull themselves up. Potties and toilet seats are usually made of plastic and you should check them regularly for splits or cracks and replace them whenever necessary.

TRAVELLING OUT AND ABOUT

In addition to keeping children safe on your premises, both indoors and out, it is also essential that you look carefully at how you will ensure a child's safety when you are out and about. Many childminders provide playgroup, nursery and school collections and take children in their care to toddler groups and other organised events. It is paramount that the children remain safe at all times whilst enjoying their time away from the home.

♦ TIP ♦

It is essential that you gain written parental permission if you are to take a child out with you and you should inform parents of any planned trips well in advance.

Cars

If you transport a child in your own car you must have prior written consent from the child's parents. You must also ensure that you and your vehicle meet the appropriate requirements:

- You must have fully comprehensive insurance which is valid for business purposes.

- Your car must be fitted with seatbelts and you must ensure that all adults in the vehicle wear a seatbelt at all times and that the children have suitable restraints appropriate for their age, weight and size.

- The doors of the vehicle must have child locks and these should be used.

- The children must have their own seat and must not be allowed to stand or travel on someone's lap.

◆ When children are getting in or out of the vehicle they must do so from the pavement side.

Public transport

If you plan to use public transport then you must ensure that:

◆ Young children are restrained with reins or wrist straps and that older children are taught to hold your hand.

◆ Children are taught how to behave on the street and to be aware of the dangers of traffic.

◆ You plan your journey in advance and know the times and places of departure of buses and trains.

◆ Children should be seated when travelling on buses or trains whenever possible. If all seats are taken make sure that children are standing safely with either a rail or you to hold on to so that they don't fall.

◆ You have a mobile telephone and contact numbers for the children in your care.

Walking

As a childminder you may spend a lot of time out walking with the children in your care. You may have several trips to the local school each day together with journeys to toddler groups, library or shops. It is important that you plan your trips carefully when out and about on foot and take into account the weather conditions and the ages and abilities of the children with you. It may not seem like a long walk to school, but if you leave the buggy at home and walk with a two year old the ten minute walk can turn out to be an hour and ten minutes splashing in puddles!

When you are out walking with the children it is a good opportunity to teach them about road safety and point out the ways that they can keep themselves safe. You can teach older children the Highway Code and encourage them to cross the road safely.

A CLEAN AND HEALTHY ENVIRONMENT

In addition to ensuring that your home is safe and free from potential dangers, it is also very important that you make sure that your home is clean and that you conform to high standards of personal hygiene. Your home will be scrutinised by many people you come across in your line of business such as parents, Ofsted inspectors, health visitors, social workers etc, and it is imperative that your home stands up to this scrutiny. You will have to demonstrate to your Ofsted inspector that you are aware of the need for high standards of hygiene and cleanliness and that you know how to prevent the spread of infection.

Washing hands

Washing hands is one of the most important and effective ways to prevent the spread of infection. Children should be encouraged to wash their hands correctly. Hands should be washed in hot water (check the temperature is not too hot) and with soap, for at least 30 seconds. Hands should always be washed:

- after visiting the toilet;
- after touching pets and their feeding bowls;
- after coughing, sneezing or blowing noses;
- after playing outside or with messy activities;
- after handling money;
- before handling food or feeding bottles and utensils;
- after changing nappies or wiping bottoms;
- when dealing with an injury.

Children and babies pick up infections easily and it is your responsibility to ensure that the environment you provide is kept thoroughly clean. In addition to good, regular cleaning it is important to provide adequate ventilation and allow fresh air and sunlight into your home whenever possible. Some of the most common places where germs and bacteria lurk are covered in the following list, and it is essential that extra care is taken to ensure that these places are cleaned thoroughly and regularly.

Changing mats and potties

These must be cleaned every time they are used. You can buy disposable changing mats although this can prove to be an expensive option if you are caring for several children in nappies. A plastic changing mat is adequate and this should be wiped down with a disinfectant solution after every nappy change. It should be replaced immediately if it becomes torn or split.

Highchairs

These should be wiped down after every use, with a suitable disinfectant solution.

Nappies and soiled clothing

Soiled nappies should be placed in a plastic bag and disposed of in an outside bin immediately. It is possible to buy specially-designed containers in which the soiled nappy is wrapped separately in an anti-bacterial film before being disposed of in a bin, but I find that scented nappy sacks with tie handles are an adequate and cost-effective way of disposing of soiled nappies efficiently and hygienically. Soiled clothing should be either rinsed and placed in a sealed bag for the parent to take home or washed according to the manufacturer's instructions immediately.

Toilets

These must be kept scrupulously clean at all times. Think carefully about the flooring around your toilet. Ideally this will be a washable surface as it is difficult to keep carpet clean and free from germs when young children are using the toilet often. Special care should be taken when cleaning the toilet as the bowl, both inside and out, the seat and the handle all need regular cleaning to avoid the spread of germs. Children should be taught to dispose of toilet paper carefully and to wash their hands after each visit to the toilet.

Soap

It is preferable to provide a liquid soap in a dispenser. This avoids cross-contamination from bars of soap used by lots of people.

Toiletries

Each child should have their own towel, face cloth, hairbrush and toothbrush. It is up to you to decide whether or not you are prepared to provide them or whether you will ask parents to provide them for their own child. For older children who are going to school, and may only be with you for a couple of hours a day, it is a good idea to provide paper towels.

Pets

Domestic animals should not be allowed near food preparation areas or where children are eating or drinking. Children should not be allowed to play near the feeding bowls belonging to pets and they should be encouraged to wash their hands after contact with animals.

ACCIDENTS AND EMERGENCIES

Despite having all the necessary safety equipment in place and following all the recommended procedures, there may still be times when accidents and emergencies occur whilst children are in your care. Obviously prevention is the best possible solution, but how you cope in an emergency situation will have far-reaching consequences on the outcome of any accidents.

Careful planning and prior preparation is essential in order to deal with any emergencies effectively. It is important to practice safety procedures regularly and to update contact details periodically so that you know exactly what to do and how to get in touch with a parent if the need arises. By thinking ahead you can be prepared for all eventualities.

In the case of an accident or emergency occurring on your premises it is vital that you stay calm and don't panic. It is important that you quickly assess the situation and minimise the risk of danger to yourself and others whilst offering reassurance. The way you handle yourself in an emergency is very important if you are to stay in control of the situation.

First aid training

In times of accidents and emergencies you will need to draw on your experience and first aid training. However, it is vital that you know your own limitations and do not attempt to carry out any emergency procedures that you are not confident and competent to do. If the injury requires medical attention this should be sought without delay so as not to further endanger the child.

It is important that you keep yourself up to date with your first aid training and that you periodically recap on what you have learnt so that you are proficient at dealing with an accident or emergency if it should occur. It is a waste of time enrolling on a first aid course if you never recap on what you have learnt and then panic at the first sign of an emergency. You should be familiar with how to put someone in the recovery position and how to treat common minor accidents which can happen to children, some of which we will look at now.

◆ TIP ◆

Remember the 'ABC' routine:
A – Airways – check the child's airway for blockages.
B – Breathing – check the child is breathing.
C – Circulation – check the child's circulation. Is there a pulse?

You must keep a fully stocked first aid box on your premises at all times and replenish any used items. I would recommend that you also have a small travel first aid kit that you can take with you when on outings.

You should have a fully-charged mobile telephone with you when out and about with the contact details of the parents logged into it. Alternatively, you should carry a small notebook or telephone book with details of contacts and loose change suitable for a public telephone in case you have to telephone parents from hospital or to inform them of any accident or injury to their child.

◆ TIP ◆

To create a safe environment for children, think of: safe surroundings + safe equipment + safe practice.

Accident	Treatment
Head injury	Place a cold object over the injury to act as a compress. Be aware of symptoms such as vomiting, drowsiness and headaches and seek medical attention if necessary.
Objects stuck in the nose or ears	Never attempt to remove the object yourself: seek medical advice immediately.
Bruises	Use a cold compress.
Sprains	Use a cold compress and elevate the sprained area.
Minor burns	Run the burn under a cold tap for a minimum of ten minutes; increase this to 20 minutes in the case of a chemical burn. Leave the burn uncovered.
Cuts and grazes	Rinse the area in clean water to ensure that the wound is completely clean and apply a suitable dressing if necessary.
Nose bleeds	Instruct the child to tip their head forward, and gently but firmly pinch the area just below the bridge of the nose.

5

Launching Your Business

CREATING THE RIGHT IMAGE

However you choose to run your business, whether you decide to work part time or full time, with another childminder or alone, is entirely up to you. However, one thing all childminders must do if they are to succeed is to portray a professional image at all times.

You are an individual who is trained in caring for children. You have specialised knowledge in all aspects of how children develop and learn and you are competent in providing stimulating activities in a safe and secure environment. Your business, and the image you give to others, should show this professionalism at all times. You are entitled to respect from the adults and the children you are providing a service for and, likewise, you must show respect in return.

You will have worked hard to get your business up and running and may have gone through many months of training and preparation waiting for your registration to go through. It is essential that you do yourself justice once you are ready to launch your business.

Ten tips for creating the right image
1. Always be ready for the children in the morning. Be organised and prepared. Working from home does not mean that it is appropriate for you to greet parents and children in your dressing gown having just crawled out of bed!

2. Always make the children and their parents feel welcome, listen to what they have to say and respect their wishes.

3. Be punctual. Never take children to playgroup, nursery or school late and make sure you are there to collect them on time.

4. Ensure that your home is clean and safe at all times.

5. Always be polite.

6. Be as helpful and flexible as possible.

7. Keep accurate, up-to-date records of all the children in your care.

8. Keep parents informed of important issues such as contract review dates, holidays, fees etc and give as much notice as possible for any changes you wish to bring about.

9. Keep up to date with your training and refresh your professional knowledge and skills whenever appropriate.

10. Always remember that you are a trained professional providing an important service and as such must act responsibly at all times when caring for children.

DECIDING ON THE KIND OF SERVICE TO PROVIDE

This may seem relatively easy but there are many different things you must take into consideration when deciding on the kind of childminding service you are going to provide. It is probably best to sit down and discuss this aspect of the business with your own partner, children or anyone else who may be affected by your duties. Think about the following points:

- Are you going to work part time or full time?
- Are you going to work weekdays and/or weekends?
- Are you going to work bank holidays?
- What are your core hours likely to be?
- Are you willing to cover early mornings or late evenings?

◆ TIP ◆

Decide early on what kind of service you are willing to provide and stick to your decision. Never agree to something you are not happy with simply to secure business – you will resent it in time.

The previous questions will not only be dependent on your own preference, but probably on your family commitments as well. Is it practical to work until 7pm if you have children of your own who need to be taken to clubs or activities during that time? Does agreeing to work weekends and/or antisocial hours conflict with the time you wish to spend with your own family?

Others factors you will need to consider are:

◆ Are you willing to take and collect children from playgroup, nursery and school?

◆ If so, which nursery, playgroup and schools are you going to concentrate on? This will have a big effect when advertising your business.

◆ Are you willing to care for older children?

◆ Are you prepared to look after babies?

◆ Do you want to work term time only or are you willing to provide school holiday care?

◆ What type of meals are you willing to provide?

◆ What type of activities and learning experiences are you able to provide, and for what age group?

Knowing your limits

You need to answer all these questions as accurately as possible. I cannot stress enough how important it is not to agree to something unless you are completely satisfied with the arrangement yourself. Once you have signed a contract and agreed to provide a service for the parent you will be obliged to stick to the arrangement until the contract is renewed or changes agreed. It is not a good idea to fill a place by making promises that you will have difficulty keeping; it will result in resentment and dissatisfied customers, both of which must be avoided at all costs.

A parent may approach you to request a one-off change to the usual conditions of their contract; for example an early morning start or late evening finish due to work commitments, and it is important that if you agree to this change, you stress that it is an exception to the contract and that you can't do it on a regular basis.

Remember, always be clear in your own mind what your limitations are and try to stick to them at all times. If you are not willing or able to do something *don't* agree to it!

It is worth bearing in mind that parents can and will put you on the spot from time to time. They may request something that you feel obliged to agree to but, after thinking about it later, you are unable to carry through. In cases like this it is best to refrain from agreeing to anything immediately but say that you will give it consideration. This way you will have the time to work out whether their request is a reasonable one and whether you can fit it around your existing obligations and family commitments. It is important to be assertive whilst remaining polite and helpful. It will not do you any favours to be inflexible and awkward but it will breed bitterness and resentment if you feel your good nature is being taken advantage of.

◆ TIP ◆

If a parent makes a request that you are not sure you can or want to meet, ask for time to think the proposal over rather than giving a spur of the moment decision that you may later come to regret.

BUILDING A PORTFOLIO

I would advise all childminders to build a portfolio about themselves and put together a small welcome pack for potential customers. It is a good idea to do this well in advance so that you are prepared when parents telephone you enquiring about your childminding services. A **portfolio** contains information about yourself and is designed for you to look at with the parents and explain its contents. A **welcome pack** is intended for the parents to take away with them to keep as a reference.

You may like to devise a booklet or leaflet about your childminding business and this can be useful to send through the post to enquiring parents prior to setting up a meeting with them.

A **portfolio** should consist of the following information:

◆ A short history about yourself, your family and your experience to date.

◆ A copy of your registration certificate.

◆ A copy of your report from Ofsted or CSIW.

◆ A copy of your police check (CRB).

◆ A copy of your first aid training certificate.

◆ Copies of any training certificates such as Introducing Childminding Practice, Developing Childminding Practice, Extending Childminding Practice, Quality Assurance, NVQ Level 3 in Childcare and Education.

◆ References from previous parents who have used your services.

◆ Sample menus.

◆ Brief details of your usual daily routine, including regular visits to toddler groups and other organisations.

◆ Your personal emergency plan.

◆ Copies of your policies.

◆ Descriptions of the activities you offer the children.

◆ Copies of your insurance policies relevant to your childminding business, for example public liability, house and contents and car insurance.

◆ Details of any workshops or seminars you have attended.

- Details of the days and times you are available to work and any holiday dates already booked – remember to update this information as and when necessary.

- Details of your fees for full and part-time attendance. This information should state what is included in the price and what parents will be expected to supply.

A portfolio should incorporate as much relevant information as possible which shows prospective parents the kind of service you provide. It should be well organised and easy to read.

A **welcome pack** should consist of the following information:

- A leaflet or booklet advertising your business.

- Details of your full name and address, including your postcode, your telephone number (both land line and mobile if you have one), and your e-mail address if you have one.

- A brief outline of your daily routine.

- A brief outline of the activities you provide.

- Details of the schools nurseries and playgroups you take and collect from.

- Details of the days and hours you are available including the dates of any holidays already booked.

- Details of your fees and what they include.

- Sample menus and details of any special diets you are able to cater for.

- A photocopy of your registration certificate and last inspection report.

- A registration document for the parents to complete before you agree to care for their child.

- Copies of any relevant policies.

You may like to add copies of your training certificates to the welcome pack but it is important not to swamp potential customers or they may end up not reading any of it!

WORKING WITH ANOTHER CHILDMINDER OR ASSISTANT

Childminding can at times be a lonely profession. You may find yourself at home for many hours with only very young children for company, particularly in the winter months when the weather is bad and it is not as easy to get out and about with toddlers and babies. If you have been used to working outside the home in the past, getting used to the loneliness and having the responsibility of being your own boss can be rather daunting.

You must be organised to run your own business, whatever your profession, and you must take responsibility for things if they go wrong. There is no one immediately at hand to turn to for support, help and advice or to share the workload. It is for these reasons, together with friendship and companionship, that some childminders opt to work with another childminder or employ an assistant to work with them. There are both advantages and disadvantages of working with someone else and we will look at some of these now.

Advantages of working with another childminder or employing an assistant

- ◆ **Adult company**: Unless you are prepared to take the children you look after to lots of different clubs or outings, which is not always practical as they can be expensive and have to fit in with the routines of the children you are caring for, then you will find yourself spending a lot of time void of adult company if you work alone. For many people, working with another adult is stimulating and makes many tasks easier. Having someone to work with who is as keen and enthusiastic as you is a great boost and it helps to be able to motivate one another.

- ◆ **Sharing views and ideas**: Working alone can result in ideas becoming stale and unadventurous. You may have had lots of ideas for activities at the outset when starting up your business but, after a while, it can be difficult to have the motivation to come up with new ideas to stimulate the children. Having another adult present means that there is the option of 'pooling' ideas. One of you may be brilliant at artwork whilst the other may have musical ability. By working together you can share your knowledge and expertise, to the benefit of the children.

◆ **Flexibility and backup**: If you work alone and you or one of your own children are ill it can mean letting parents down if you are not able to go about your childminding duties. Working with another childminder or employing an assistant can help overcome this obstacle as there are always two people available. (Obviously you must still adhere to the conditions of your registration and not exceed the number of children one of you can care for alone.)

◆ **Reassurance**: We all need reassurance at times and it is good to have someone there to share the trials and tribulations that running your own business can bring. There may be times when a parent is being unreasonable or is unhappy about a particular situation, and it is always good to be able to seek impartial advice from someone else. (Remember that it is important to respect your settings' confidentiality procedures before discussing certain things with an assistant.)

◆ **Emergencies**: Having another adult present in times of accidents, illnesses or emergencies can be very helpful. It is much easier to stay calm and in control of the situation if you have help readily available. By working as a team you will be able to manage any emergency situation much more easily and, should a trip to the hospital be necessary, you don't have the added problem of finding someone to care for the other children you are minding.

◆ **Adult:child ratios increased**: By working with another childminder or employing an assistant the number of children you are registered to care for would be increased. The exact number of children is determined by Ofsted.

◆ **Shared costs**: Obviously the everyday costs of providing food and drink would not be reduced as you will probably be caring for a larger number of children if you are working with another childminder, but the cost of purchasing equipment should be considerably less as you can share the cost of toys and resources.

Disadvantages of working with another childminder or assistant

◆ **Authority**: It may be difficult to determine who has overall authority when important decisions are being made. If you are working with another childminder disputes could arise, for example, depending on whose house the business is run from. If you employ an assistant you must be confident at giving clear, concise instructions and make sure the assistant is aware of exactly what is expected of them.

- **Differences in work attitude**: Problems may arise if you and the person you are working with have very different attitudes regarding the way you wish to run the business. Whilst one of you may be willing to improve your skills through training courses, the other may not be prepared to give up their free time in this way and resentment may arise. It must be made clear for everyone involved, prior to starting the business, what is expected from each individual.

- **Friendships**: Friendships can suffer when two people spend long hours together day after day. You may think that you have a solid friendship but tempers can become frayed when faced with the very demanding job of caring for young children.

- **Working out wages, expenses etc**: It may seem fair to split the profits of the business equally if you are working with another childminder and pay an equal proportion of the cost of purchasing toys, equipment, food and drink, but who will be responsible for calculating how much heating, lighting, gas/electricity for cooking, toilet rolls and soap are being used? Who will be expected to wash and iron the extra towels and bedding? These are all questions which need to be addressed fairly if your business is to succeed.

If you employ an assistant and pay wages you will be responsible for Income Tax and National Insurance payments and you must be aware of, and comply with, the employment law in these cases. You will be expected to pay your employee the minimum wage which currently stands at £4.85 per hour for anyone over the age of 22 and £4.10 for anyone aged 18 to 21. Changes to the national minimum wage which took place in October 2004 now means that 16 and 17 year olds are entitled to a minimum hourly rate of £3.00. As an employer you will also need to have employer's liability insurance in addition to public liability insurance.

◆ **TIP** ◆

Think carefully before agreeing to employ an assistant or work with another childminder. Friendships can suffer due to long hours in each others' company and you must be sure that you both have the same aims, otherwise one of you may end up doing all the work whilst the other simply enjoys the benefits!

Whether you decide to work alone, employ an assistant or work with another childminder is up to you. What I would recommend, if you are thinking of working with someone else, is to think very carefully about what you want and how you see your business developing. Work out, in detail, how you are going to calculate your expenditure and organise your accounts. Make sure *all* parties are happy with the arrangements prior to commencing the business and never agree to anything initially that you feel you may resent later on.

ADVERTISING

In order for your childminding business to be successful and for you to make an income you need to keep your places full. Although your food bills may be lower if you care for fewer children, other expenses such as heating, lighting and insurance will remain the same and it is therefore important that you address any vacancies you may have. There are many factors that will dictate whether or not you need to advertise your services, such as whether there is a lot of competition in your area.

Some childminders find they never have to advertise their services and actually have waiting lists. This is by far the best position to be in but it is usually the case for well-established childminders who have built up a lot of contacts. Well-established childminders tend to get a lot of recommendations and this is one of the best ways to get business. It is a great compliment for a childminder to be recommended by someone who has, or is, using their services as no one is going to recommend a childminder that they themselves are not happy with! If you find yourself with vacancies and are unsure of how to go about filling them it is worth considering the following:

Tell people

Mention to your local schools, playgroups and nurseries that you are a registered childminder and ask them if they would consider putting a poster on their notice board or a couple of leaflets in their reception area offering your services.

Put up a notice

Put a card or notice in your local shop window, library, doctors' surgery or baby clinic. It is important to make a good impression at this stage so make sure that any posters, leaflets or cards you distribute are clear and concise and that they state legibly the service you are offering. Try to incorporate an eye-catching design. Make sure that you do not put your address on any advertising material as you may find yourself attracting unwanted responses. It should be sufficient to put your name and contact number so that potential customers can get in touch to discuss the service they require prior to visiting. Opposite is an example of a leaflet you could use to advertise your business.

Posting leaflets

If there is a new housing development in your area with homes targeting families, it may be a good idea to spend some time posting leaflets or brochures through their letterboxes. Families who are new to the area may not be aware of the childminding services available and by making the initial contact you may be removing any potential competition.

Children's Information Service

Contact your local Children's Information Service. These offices keep lists of registered childminders and provide details of childminders who have vacancies to parents who make enquiries. The CIS will also put your details on the internet, with your permission.

Share details

Other childminders in your area can prove helpful in filling your vacancies. Often if a childminder receives an enquiry that they can't help with they are happy to give out other local childminder details. I

REGISTERED CHILDMINDER HAS A FULL-TIME VACANCY

For one child aged between 2 and 5 years

Available from 3 January 200X – Monday to Friday

▶ **7 years' experience**

▶ **Registered with Ofsted**

▶ **Level 3 NVQ**

▶ **Level 3 Certificate in Childminding Practice**

▶ **First Aid trained**

▶ **Competitive rates**

▶ **References available**

▶ **Local school, nursery and playgroup collections**

▶ **School holiday cover available**

For more information, please contact

(YOUR NAME AND TELEPHONE NUMBER)

have certainly found that people are very grateful if you can put them in touch with other childminding businesses.

Childminding groups

If you are a member of a local childminding group you should ask if they have a list of childminders with vacancies. Lots of areas have a childminding co-ordinator and if this is the case in your area you need to inform her that you have vacancies.

Local newspaper

Some childminders choose to advertise their services in local newspapers. However, be very cautious about how you word your advert. Experience has taught me that very few prospective customers choose their childminders in this way and, in addition to the expense of newspaper advertising, you may find yourself receiving unwanted responses. *Never* print your address in a newspaper advertising that you care for young children.

If you do decide that a newspaper advertisement is for you then keep your advert short and to the point; remember you will be charged for the amount of lines you use and you should stick to the important points.

Phone directories

It may be possible for some childminders to obtain a free entry in the *Yellow Pages* (your name and telephone number) under the childminder section. Telephone 0808 100 8182 for further details. It may also be possible for you to obtain a free entry in the *Thomson Local* (name and telephone number). Telephone 01252 555 555 for details.

◆ TIP ◆

Keep your advertisements short and stick to the important points. If you are paying, ask for a lineage advertisement in the 'Childminding' section.

INTERVIEWING POTENTIAL CUSTOMERS

The first meeting you have with a parent is extremely important. This is the time when potential customers make a decision as to whether to place their child in your care or not. Everything will depend on how you conduct the interview and the impression you make. You will need to be confident without being arrogant, assertive without being aggressive and efficient without being inflexible.

It is important that the parents feel they can talk to you and ask you as many questions as they feel necessary. You should always make sure that you have plenty of time to interview prospective parents, and the first meeting should, ideally, be when you are not caring for any other children so that you can devote this time to the family in question. Remember that *you* are interviewing *them* just as much as *they* are interviewing *you*.

First impressions are very important. Have your information portfolio and welcome pack available and think of a few simple activities you can get ready for the child so that they can be entertained whilst you discuss the childcare arrangements with the parents.

THE FIRST MEETING

The first meeting is a good time for an informal chat. It is your opportunity to sell your business. You may feel anxious about this meeting, particularly if this is your first interview with prospective customers. You need to prepare yourself and try to anticipate the kind of questions you may be asked and have your answers ready. (See the section on Frequently Asked Questions at the end of this chapter.)

◆ TIP ◆

> First impressions are crucial. Often a parent will make up their minds about the service you provide within the first few minutes of meeting you.

At this initial meeting it is a good idea to show the parents the rooms where you carry out your childminding business. Explain your usual daily routines and the kinds of activities you provide. If you have an outdoor space which you use for childminding, show this to the parents as well. Show your personal portfolio and tell them about your training and qualifications. Explain your procedure for settling in and the paperwork involved.

It is important to be friendly whilst professional. Parents need to know that you are confident in the work that you do but also need to feel that they can approach you to ask for information whenever necessary.

Remembering your limits

At this stage, *never* agree to something you know you cannot do just to get custom. For example, if you already provide a school collection service to one school, never agree to take or collect from another school simply to attract potential customers if this will mean that you are late to either or both of the schools. If you are intending to service more than one school it is essential that you know the opening and closing times of the schools so that you are there when the children are let out – never have children hanging around the playground or streets waiting for you.

The initial meeting will be the time when both you and the parents will decide whether the service you provide will be suitable for the child. Of course it is necessary to be flexible in your approach, but if you are intending to finish work at 5.30pm in order to fit in with other commitments, it is important that you do not agree, at this stage, to work until 6.00pm if you know that you will resent this later on.

◆ TIP ◆

The initial meeting is not just an opportunity for parents to decide whether they like you; it is also a chance for you to decide whether or not you could work with the family.

Making a decision

Unless you are completely sure that you can care for the child and feel able to communicate well with the parents after the first meeting, I would never advise signing the contract on the initial meeting. I would recommend that you give the parents the information pack and all the details they require. Ask them to think things over and perhaps agree a time for them to telephone you in a couple of days with their decision. This gives you both time to reflect on the interview and decide whether or not you feel that you could work together.

I advise prospective customers to look at other childminding settings, before making up their minds, so that they are aware of the other options available and can be sure that they have chosen the right childminder for their needs. Agreeing to speak again in a couple of days gives the parents the chance to look at other settings, if they wish, and talk things over together privately, with their child if necessary, before getting back to you with a decision. It also gives you time to reflect on the arrangements the parents have requested and whether or not it is possible for you to agree to them.

SETTLING A CHILD IN

If the parents come back to you with a favourable decision and you feel confident that you can provide the service they require, then you should arrange a further meeting to negotiate the contract and make arrangements for settling the child into your setting.

Getting to know the child
Sometimes it will be necessary to take a child on at very short notice and therefore not possible to arrange short visits prior to the contract commencing. If this is the case, then it is vital that you request as much information about the child as possible from their parents, in order that you can help the child get used to you and your setting with as little disruption as possible. Remember, the more you know about a child, the easier it will be to know what makes them happy, apprehensive or sad.

Short sessions
Ideally, you will have the opportunity to get to know the child and for them to get to know you through a series of short sessions at your setting. If a mother is on maternity leave for example, it is a fantastic opportunity for you to arrange to care for their baby for perhaps an hour initially, building this up to two or three hours over a period of several weeks. This gives you the chance to get to know the baby, it gives the baby the chance to get used to being away from his mother and it gets the mother used to being away from her child – all very important if you are to make caring for the child a success.

Try to ensure that you arrange to care for the baby for some of the feeds during the settling in period. Some babies, particularly those that have only ever been breastfed, find it very difficult to take feeds from a stranger and it is vital that any feeding problems are addressed prior to the mother returning to work and leaving the baby in your full-time care.

Older children can be helped to settle into the setting if you take the time beforehand to get to know which activities they particularly enjoy and what their interests are.

Difficulties settling

Children vary immensely in their response to coping with new environments. Whilst some children will not have any difficulty separating from their parents and will rise to the challenges a new setting has to offer, others may find it difficult to settle. There are several ways to help a child who may be experiencing difficulty settling with you:

◆ **Visit the child in their own home** so that they can get used to you on their own terms and in the security of an environment they are happy in.

◆ **Arrange for short, regular visits** to your home prior to the placement beginning.

◆ **Encourage the parent to stay** with the child for an extended period of time, gradually reducing the amount of time they stay, perhaps over a period of weeks.

◆ **Suggest that the child brings a couple of treasured toys** or a comforter from home that they can turn to for reassurance whenever necessary.

When the time comes for the parent to leave the setting, encourage them to do so as quickly as possible. Children can become more and more distressed if the goodbyes are drawn out. However, don't encourage parents to 'sneak off' while their child is busy doing something else; this can lead to insecurity and distrust.

Once the parent has left try to devote as much time and attention to the child as possible and provide activities which you know they are familiar with and enjoy doing. These activities should not be too demanding and should not take too much concentration or effort.

◆ **TIP** ◆

Encourage parents to resist the temptation to prolong the farewell. Long, drawn-out farewells can be stressful to everyone and you should encourage the parents to keep their goodbyes short.

FREQUENTLY ASKED QUESTIONS

It is a good idea to prepare yourself before any meetings with potential customers. The interview is the time when parents want to question you about the service you provide and it is a good idea to be prepared for these questions so that you can answer confidently. Some of the questions asked frequently by prospective customers are:

- What are your opening hours?
- What fees do you charge?
- Which schools, nurseries, playgroups do you service?
- What activities do you provide?
- How will you fit in with my baby's established routine?
- Where will my child sleep?
- What kinds of meals do you provide?
- Will you be taking my child out in a car?
- What are your accident and emergency procedures?
- How many children are you registered to care for?
- Do you have access to a library and, if so, do you take the children?

The first meeting is also an opportunity for you to ask questions and these may be along the following lines:

- What days/hours will you require?
- Does your child have any special dietary requirements?
- Are you able to make arrangements for the collection of the child if you are going to be late?
- Are you able to make alternative arrangements for the child if they are unwell and therefore unable to attend?
- Will the child require taking to/collecting from playgroup, nursery or school?

6

Negotiating a Contract

DECIDING HOW MUCH TO CHARGE

This is probably one of the most difficult decisions you will make when starting out in your childminding business. Charge too much and you will struggle to fill your vacancies, charge too little and you will not get the financial rewards appropriate for a highly skilled professional job.

◆ TIP ◆

Childminding is a highly skilled career and the fees you charge should reward your expertise.

Childminding often means long hours and demanding work and the fees you charge should reflect this. It is often assumed that, as you work from home, you do not have overheads as such to think about but this is not true. You have additional costs and there are a number of things you ought to consider before deciding what to charge.

When setting your fees you must take into account your everyday business expenses for example heating and lighting, wear and tear on your home, public liability insurance, food and drink, toilet rolls, toys, books and play equipment. It is usual for all of these costs to be included in the basic fee. By making a list of all your usual expenses you will be able to calculate how much you spend on a weekly, monthly or annual basis and incorporate these costs into your fees.

For example:

Annual costs	Weekly costs
Registration fee payable to Ofsted.	Food and drink purchased for the children you are childminding.
Public liability and household insurance.	Wages for yourself and any assistant you may employ, including NIC and income tax.
National Childminding Association membership fee (if applicable).	Items such as paper, paints, craft materials etc.
Training costs for professional development including first aid training.	Travel expenses incurred whilst carrying out your childminding duties, such as petrol to take the children to clubs, schools etc.
Wear and tear on premises and equipment.	The cost of activities, outings and treats.
Heat, light, water etc – increased household bills.	
Equipment and toys.	
Christmas presents for the children you care for in your childminding work.	
Birthday cards and gifts for the children you care for in your childminding work.	

♦ **Your daily expenses.** Meals, snacks and drinks will all need to be purchased and your fees should take this into account. You should be left with a reasonable amount of money after deducting your expenses otherwise you will effectively be working for nothing.

♦ **The number of hours a child will be with you.** Will you charge a different rate for hourly, daily or full-time attendance?

♦ **Your qualifications and experience.** Some parents are willing to pay more for an experienced childminder who has gained lots of qualifications; others are not swayed by this as their own earning potential often dictates how much they can afford to pay for childcare.

♦ **The fees other childminders in your area are charging.** These childminders are your competition and it is not a good idea to charge more for your service unless you can offer a significantly different or specialised service. Undercutting your fellow childminders may mean you get the customers but you will be doing yourself a disservice and alienating yourself from those you may wish to be friends with, and who may also attend your local toddler and support groups.

◆ **Restriction of numbers.** You will be restricted by the number of children you are registered to mind and you should bear this in mind.

◆ **Are you going to offer discounts** for siblings or advance payments?

◆ **Are your fees inclusive** of bank holidays and holiday pay?

◆ Are you intending to charge more for babies than older school-aged children?

◆ **Term-time opening.** Are you only looking after school-aged children during term time? If this is the case, think of the 13 weeks plus per annum when schools are closed for holidays or training days and your earning potential may be drastically reduced.

◆ **The demand for the service in your area.** This will have a great impact on the fees you will be able to charge. A high level of unemployment, for example, will reduce the number of people seeking a childminder as opposed to families where both parents are in full-time employment.

◆ Bear in mind how much Working Tax Credit and Child Tax Credit parents can claim when deciding what fees to charge. You can find more information about tax credits by contacting the Inland Revenue.

◆ **TIP** ◆

Never fall into the trap of agreeing to care for children as a favour for friends or family. Set your fees and stick to them, or you may find yourself losing money and ultimately going out of business!

CHARGING FOR EXTRAS

You must decide, when setting your hourly/daily/weekly rates, what the fee will include and what you expect parents to pay for in addition. You must make it clear to parents whether the basic fee includes cooked or cold meals and which meals and snacks you are going to provide. In addition to your usual everyday costs you can incorporate additional expenses and these should be agreed with the parents prior to commencement of the contract. Some of these extras may include:

Nappies

Will you request that the parent provides their own or pays you for them, at cost, as and when used? Remember, parents may have a preference for a particular brand of nappies. If you care for two or three children who are still wearing nappies you could be shelling out a substantial amount of money on nappies alone not to mention the space required to store several packs. If a child leaves your setting you could be left with a stock of nappies which are surplus to requirements and which you may not be able to use for some time.

I have always found it practical to request that parents provide their own toiletry requisites including nappies, but I also ensure that I have a small stock available for emergencies. If you have the storage space, ask the parent to provide a full pack of nappies and let them know when stocks are low and you need further supplies. This eliminates the need for busy parents to remember to pack a fresh supply every day.

Formula milk

Like nappies, each parent will have a preference as to the brand of formula milk they require and babies must not be moved from one formula to another. I would therefore always advise childminders to request that parents provide their own formula milk. This can be done with the parents providing the milk in powder form or, if preferred, already made up in bottles.

Food items for special diets

This is purely down to preference. If you are caring for a child who requires certain food items due to a special diet it is up to you and the parents to decide which items are needed and who will pay for them. It is unlikely that costs will be higher when catering for a vegetarian diet and so extra charges would not usually apply in this case. If, however, you make your own baby foods and a parent requests that their child is fed only prepared shop-bought jars, or powdered food, then it is perfectly acceptable to ask them either to provide the food themselves or pay for the jars you provide. (I would advise that you keep all your receipts if you choose this option.)

Regular long car journeys

If you have agreed to transport a child to a particular nursery, school or club which incorporates a long journey by car you would not normally make, then it is reasonable to charge for petrol. This should be agreed with the parent prior to commencement of the contract.

Special outings

Childminders often take children out and about and many trips do not incorporate extra charges. However, before planning any special outings you should agree with the parents who will be responsible for things such as entrance fees, bus fares, ice cream etc.

◆ TIP ◆

Always make it clear to parents what the standard fee includes and which items they will be expected to pay extra for.

AGREED HOURS

It is vital that you agree how many hours are included in the basic fee you charge. If, for example, a parent is paying for three hours at an agreed hourly rate for before and after school care but regularly brings their child earlier or collects later than the agreed times then you should request a review of the contracted hours to incorporate the extra hours worked. Often the parent will see the error of their ways and revert to the original contracted hours rather than pay an additional fee, but the problem will have been resolved and you will no longer be working overtime, free of charge.

It is very important that parents understand and agree which hours are included in the basic fee and what charges, if any, you propose to make for additional hours. Some childminders do not charge for occasional extra hours whilst others set a higher rate for hours worked outside those specified in the contract. Whatever you choose, make sure that you stick to your decision. If you do not want to work unsocial hours, weekends or bank holidays make sure you state this before commencement of the contract to avoid any misunderstandings later on.

SETTLING IN PERIODS

It can take some time for the relationship between a child, childminder and parents to settle down. A settling in period of two to four weeks is an acceptable length of time for a child, parent and carer to decide whether the relationship is a happy one or not. If a contract is terminated during the settling in period by either party it is reasonable for the childminder to keep any retainer fees (see below) they may have been paid but this is a matter of preference, and may well depend on the circumstances surrounding the end of the placement. You must make sure that parents are fully aware of how they stand with regard to any retainer fees paid, prior to commencement of the contract.

RETAINER FEES

If a parent asks to reserve a place which could be offered to another child who could take up the place immediately then you may choose to charge a retainer fee.

As you are limited by your registration to the number of children you can care for, you will lose income if you hold a place open for a child and turn others away. Often a parent who has just had a baby, but is still on maternity leave, will spend this time looking at potential childcare options for when they return to work. When they find a childminder they like they may request that a place is held for their child. A retainer fee can be charged for the weeks you are waiting for the child to start.

How much you decide to charge as a retainer is entirely up to you and should be negotiated with the parent. A large proportion of childminders charge half the usual fee. Retainer fees can be kept if the parent changes their mind about taking up the place, but if you are unable to offer a place when it is needed or if the terms and conditions of the agreed placement change, you should refund any retainers paid.

When to charge a retainer

Retainers should only be charged if you have a place available and are keeping that place open specifically for the child concerned. If a child is due to move on from your setting at a date which coincides with a new child's starting date, effectively making a space available for the new child, retainers should not be charged until the original contract is terminated and a place is available. You can not charge two separate families for the same place.

When deciding on charging retainers it is useful to bear the following points in mind:

- ◆ A retainer must not be charged for a baby prior to the birth.

- ◆ A retainer fee is not a credit to be deducted from childminding fees once the contract commences.

- ◆ If your circumstances change, and you are no longer able to offer the agreed service, then any retainers must be repaid to the parent.

- ◆ If a parent does not take up the place you are holding you do not have to repay the retainer fees.

- ◆ The place being retained must always be available when a retainer is charged and the place can be used at times agreed by the parent and childminder.

- ◆ Reduced retainer fees should be increased to full fee when the child takes up the place, either permanently or periodically.

◆ **TIP** ◆

A retainer fee can only be charged for a place which is available and ready to be used. You can not charge a retainer for a place which is being used by someone else.

DEPOSITS

A deposit is a one-off payment which shows that a parent intends to take up a place. A deposit is paid to secure a place which will be available on a date agreed by the parent and childminder. As with retainers, if you are unable to provide a place or you vary the agreed terms and conditions then the deposit should be refunded. Deposits are not usually repaid if the parent decides not to take up the place.

Deposits are usually refunded when the child starts by deducting the amount from the agreed childminding fees.

CHILDMINDER'S HOLIDAYS

As a self-employed person you are not automatically entitled to paid time off. However everyone needs a holiday to recharge their batteries and you will work better if you take a break at some point.

How much, if any, you decide to charge for your holiday is entirely up to you, and this should be agreed with the parents of the children you are providing care for. Whilst some childminders charge full for two–four weeks' annual holiday others charge half, as they do not have any actual expenses during the time they are not working. There are some childminders who do not charge at all when they are on holiday as their service is unavailable and they realise that parents may need to make alternative arrangements. It is possible to incorporate holiday fees in the usual hourly rate but obviously this money will be 'lost' in your weekly/ monthly payments and it is up to you to save for your holiday periods.

PARENTS' HOLIDAYS

It is important that you agree, prior to a placement commencing, how many weeks' holiday the parent will be taking each year and what they will be expected to pay. Whilst most parents and childminders try to coincide their holidays in order to cause as little disruption as possible to their own, and their child's, routine there are cases when a parent has a much higher holiday entitlement and these situations need careful consideration.

Dealing with longer holidays

If you are caring for a child whose parent is a school teacher, for example, they will probably have a minimum of 13 weeks' holiday per annum. If they choose to keep their child at home rather than bring them to you, you could be losing a lot of income. You must explain this to the parent and decide together the best course of action. You may agree to charge a retainer fee of, say, half the usual cost, but you must bear in mind that this still means a considerable loss of earnings for you. It may be possible that you can fill the place, perhaps with an older child who is also on holiday from school but whose parents do have to work.

You must think very carefully before agreeing to hold a place open for such a long time because, although sometimes it is nice to have a quiet period with fewer children to care for, this is not always a suitable option financially. It may be an idea to agree with the parent that you share the care of the child during school holidays so that you can still carry on earning but, of course, this will depend purely on preference and circumstances.

You should also bear in mind that if a child is being cared for jointly by parents who have divorced or separated, they may each have up to six weeks' annual holiday and wish to care for the child themselves during this time. This adds up to 12 weeks per annum between them and can mean a considerable loss of earnings for you.

BANK HOLIDAYS

When negotiating a contract it is important that you stipulate which, if any, bank holidays you are prepared to work. This may depend on your own personal circumstances as well as the occupations of the parents whose children you care for. Obviously some parents will never need to work bank holidays and therefore your services will not be required; others such as doctors, nurses, police and fire officers will work shifts throughout the year and will need childcare which reflects this. It is important to discuss whether or not you will work bank holidays and, if so, how much you will charge for them. Some childminders charge a higher rate and this must be negotiated prior to commencement of the contract.

Other festival days

It is also important to consider and agree which holidays and festivals you are going to recognise and work together with the parents regarding this. For example, not all cultures celebrate Christmas or Easter but if you are not willing to work on these days you must ensure that the parents are aware of it. Likewise other festivals throughout the year may be celebrated by the families of a child you care for, and if they do not attend your setting during these times you must agree the fee to be paid.

ILLNESS

Child/parent illness

It is important that parents understand that you have the right to refuse to care for a sick child. There will be times when a child is slightly 'under the weather' perhaps with a cold, earache etc, and it is usual that a childminder will be expected to continue to care for them.

However you will sometimes have to use your professional judgement to determine whether or not it is practical, and in the best interests of all the children in your setting, to agree to care for a child who is unwell. Obviously if a child has an infectious disease then you must refuse to care for them as they pose a risk to yourself and the other children you are looking after.

Payment for absences

It is important that you agree what is expected of parents, in the way of payment, should their child be ill and away from your setting. Some childminders charge half of the usual fee whilst others request full payment as the place is available for use and cannot be filled. It is also worth bearing in mind that if a parent is away from the work place because they are ill, they may prefer to keep their child with them, and you must ensure that they are aware of what fee will be payable in such cases.

Childminder illness

There may be times when either you or a member of your family is ill with an infectious disease; if this is the case you will not be able to carry out your childminding duties due to the risk of spreading infection. You must inform the parents of the children as soon as possible so that they can make alternative arrangements. It is important that you agree, prior to commencement of the contract what fees, if any, the parent will be expected to pay if you are unable to provide childcare.

On the whole I have always found that parents are receptive to paying childcare fees *whenever the place is available*. Most parents understand that you are running a business and as such have overheads and expenses to pay, regardless of whether they need to use your service or not.

◆ TIP ◆

As a general rule, if your service is available you should be charging for the place regardless of whether it is being used or not, unless you have made alternative arrangements with the parent.

RESPONSIBILITY FOR PAYMENT

It is important to decide how you expect to be paid. I would always recommend that you request parents to pay you in advance either weekly or monthly. You should agree, prior to signing the contract, when you expect payment to be made and what, if any, penalties will be incurred for late payment. Some childminders charge a one-off payment of perhaps £5 or £10 on top of the usual fee for late payment. It must be made clear to parents that you are running a professional business and that, like them, you expect to be paid on time for the service you are providing. If you do not get paid you must inform parents that you are not prepared to continue to offer your services until they have settled up with you in full. It is important that you never let arrears get out of hand. It is much easier to recoup your fees when they are relatively low than when they have spiralled out of control.

You must agree with the parents who will be responsible for the payment of your fees. Whenever possible I would advise that you arrange for both parents to be responsible for payment so that you are covered for all eventualities. For example, if only one parent has accepted responsibility for paying and that particular parent becomes unemployed or separates from the other parent, then you may find yourself going unpaid. (Obviously there will be cases when this is not a viable option, for example if the parents are divorced and one is no longer in contact with the child.)

◆ TIP ◆

Wherever possible try to ensure that *both* parents have responsibility for the payment of fees.

PLAYGROUP, NURSERY, AND CLUBS

Parents may decide to send their child to a playgroup, nursery or club in addition to using your childminding service and, if this is the case, you must agree with them who will pay for any extra charges and whether or not you will require payment when the child is not in your setting.

It is usual for childminders to continue to charge for the place if the child attends any of the above, during their contracted hours with you, and I would always recommend that you make parents aware that any extra fees for their child to attend playgroup or other clubs are payable by *them*. If you agree to pay these fees from your own income you could find yourself out of pocket as they are likely to cost more than the hourly rate you charge.

If your presence is not required at a nursery or playgroup you should still charge for the time the child is away from your setting as it is likely that you will be 'on call' during this time for example if the child is unwell, or if the nursery or playgroup is closed. At times such as these you will be expected to have a place for the child.

After-school clubs

If you provide care for school-aged children they may, from time to time, have the opportunity to attend various after-school activities such as sports, dance or learning a foreign language. You should continue to charge for the hours the child is away from your setting. These clubs are usually run for a set number of weeks after which the child will return to your setting. During the time the child is attending these clubs you will be expected to retain a place for when the course ends or if the club is cancelled due to adverse weather conditions, illness etc.

Occasionally parents may not be happy that they are expected to pay for your services if their child is not present, particularly if the child is attending a club which incorporates a further fee, and in this case you should politely explain that you are keeping a place open for their child and that you should not be expected to be out of pocket if they choose to go elsewhere for a period of time.

MATERNITY LEAVE

Many problems can arise when a parent, who is currently using your service, goes on maternity leave. It is essential that you negotiate beforehand what you are willing to accept.

You must bear in mind that maternity leave can be quite lengthy and if the mother opts to extend the basic leave they may be away from the workplace for up to a year, during which time your earning potential could be drastically reduced. Not all childminders can afford this drop in income and if you are being expected to hold two or more places open during the maternity leave period you must negotiate a suitable agreement that works for both parties involved. You may decide to charge a retainer or a reduced weekly fee.

Negotiating a fee

If a parent who is already using your services wishes to keep the child who usually attends your setting with her, you must agree together what fee you will expect. It is reasonable for you to charge a retainer fee for this period of time and perhaps agree to provide occasional care so that the child's routine is not disrupted too much.

There are many factors to bear in mind when deciding what to charge when a parent is on maternity leave. The mother may decide not to return to work when the time comes, or if she does return it may be on a part-time basis. If you have spent many months on a reduced rate expecting it to be increased when the mother's maternity leave is over you could feel resentful if she changes her plans. In some cases, it may be advisable to terminate the existing contract and, if a suitable compromise cannot be agreed, you may need to ask the parent to re-apply for a place when she is in a position to return to work. This will of course depend on your availability at the time.

CARING FOR CHILDREN FROM THE SAME FAMILY

Many childminders recognise the expense faced by working parents having to pay for childcare for two or more children and agree to offer a discount in these cases. However, it is important that you realise that although you may be earning less money, your overheads will remain the same if you are caring for siblings. Before agreeing to a discount you must work out your overheads and ensure that accepting less payment will not mean a cut in standards of care and the facilities you provide.

If you decide to offer a discount it is important that you make the parent aware of what you expect them to pay if one of the children is absent due to illness, and what the full fee will be if one of the children leaves your setting, perhaps when they start school or become older teenagers and are able to go home from school on their own. It is important that any discounts offered when two or more siblings are in your care are not automatically expected when the number of children attending from the same family decreases.

SIGNING THE CONTRACT

Before signing a contract it is vital that all parties involved are aware that they are committing themselves to a legally binding document and as such everyone must understand exactly what they are agreeing to. It is essential that any questions and queries are cleared up before signing a contract.

Content of the contract

The contract should clearly state the following:

◆ The details of the childminder including their name, address, telephone number, registration number and public liability insurance details.

◆ The details of the child to be cared for and their parents including names, addresses and telephone numbers.

◆ The details of any other person who may be asked to drop off or collect the child from your setting.

◆ Access arrangements if the parents are separated or divorced.

◆ Any special requirements including preferences, likes and dislikes.

◆ The usual days, times and hours the child will require care.

◆ Details of payment including hourly/weekly/monthly rates, dates for payment and any penalty clauses incurred for late payment.

◆ Details of holiday/illness/occasional care required and the fees payable.

◆ Details of any out-of-school clubs, playgroup, nursery attendances.

◆ Details of the items which are included in the fee and which items you expect the parent to either provide or pay extra for.

◆ Details of any retainers or deposits payable.

◆ If appropriate, details regarding settling-in periods.

When, and only when, you and the parents are completely happy with the contents of the contract you should sign and date it.

I would advise all childminders to become a member of the National Childminding Association (NCMA). Through them you can purchase contracts that cover all the important aspects of your childminding business. If you do choose to devise your own contract it is important that you make sure that you have covered all eventualities in case of any disputes later on and that you write it clearly to avoid misinterpretation or misunderstanding.

◆ TIP ◆

A contract is a legally binding agreement and it is vital that all parties completely understand what is expected of them prior to signing.

Additional information required

At the same time as signing the contract you should ask the parents to complete a child record form – also available from NCMA – giving details about the child and any special requirements they may have. In addition, the form requests details about the child's parents including their place of work and contact numbers. You should also obtain details of other contacts for use in the case of an emergency when perhaps it is not possible to get hold of the parent at very short notice. The child's personal details, including doctor and health visitor together with immunisation and health history, should also be recorded.

REVIEWING THE CONTRACT

There should be space on your contract for details of a review. At the time of signing it is advisable to inform the parents that the contract will be enforced from the date of commencement of the placement until, say, twelve months later, when you will review the terms and conditions. If circumstances change before the twelve months is at an end then obviously the review date must be brought forward. It is important to remind parents when the review date is coming up and to set yourself time to decide what, if any, changes need to be made to the contract. Most childminders use this review date to increase their fees.

◆ TIP ◆

It is a good idea to make a note in your diary of when each contract is coming up for renewal as you will have different contract dates for each family.

TERMINATING THE CONTRACT

Your contract should include a termination clause which clearly states the amount of notice required by both parties should a contract be terminated. The usual amount of notice is between two and four weeks. Anything less than two weeks may make it difficult for the parents to arrange alternative childcare and could also mean that you have a vacancy left open with little time to fill it. Anything more than four weeks could be awkward, depending on the reasons why the contract is being terminated. It could also make it difficult for you to fill the vacancy if there is a lengthy wait for the place to become free. Notice of termination should be given in writing and this should not include any arranged holiday periods.

The notice period applies to all parties involved in the contract and you must continue to ensure that your service is available as stated in your agreed contract. If the parents decide to end the contract and immediately withdraw the child from your care then they must pay your fees in lieu of the notice stated within the contract. It is worth remembering that if you refuse to care for a child during the notice period stated on the contract then you are also liable to pay the parents' fees in lieu of notice. They may then decide to take you to the small claims court to claim further costs against you as a result of your refusing to provide care under the terms of the contract. They may try to recover costs such as loss of earnings, if one parent has had to take time off work until alternative childcare arrangements can be made, and you should bear this in mind.

◆ TIP ◆

A contract remains in force until such a time that it is terminated or renewed.

7

Accounts and Bookkeeping

As a childminder you are classed as self-employed and as such it is important for you to know about the financial side of running a small business. Many people are worried about the paperwork involved in running a business and it is vital that you organise your accounts in a professional way. In this chapter we will look at the important issues surrounding accounts for small businesses.

YOUR RESPONSIBILITIES

Working as a 'self-employed' childminder means that you are not actually employed by the parents of the children you care for, and as such you are responsible for your own income tax and national insurance payments. You are contracted to the parents at a rate agreed by both parties. As you do not actually work for anyone you have sole responsibility for the following:

♦ Maintaining accurate, up-to-date, financial records which show your income and expenditure.

♦ Paying for insurance to cover yourself, your home and your car.

♦ Obtaining legal and public liability insurance.

♦ Paying income tax and national insurance contributions for yourself.

Keeping the tax office informed
It is important that you inform your local tax office that you are a registered childminder and that you are earning an income working from home. You must provide this information regardless of whether you are earning sufficient money to pay tax or not. If you are not liable to

pay tax, you must still keep accurate records to ensure that you are in a position to prove your income and expenditure should this be necessary.

Small businesses, including childminders, with a turnover of less than £15,000 per annum are not required by law to employ the services of an accountant. However, the Inland Revenue will require you to supply details of your:

◆ total income for the year;

◆ total expenditure for the year;

◆ net profit for the year.

Self-assessment

The rules for self-assessment require you to:

◆ Inform the Inland Revenue that you are working.

◆ Ensure that you have an organised system for keeping accurate records.

◆ Keep these records up to date.

◆ Retain these records for six years.

Your records must include details of any money you have received for your work as a childminder, together with any money you have spent in relation to your business. It is, of course, entirely up to you how you decide to keep your accounts. There is no set way, and it is very much a matter of personal preference.

KEEPING ON TOP OF THINGS

However, what you must make sure is that your records are accurate and up to date. I can not stress enough how important it is to do your accounts on a *weekly* or *monthly* basis. This avoids a backlog in accounts and ensures that income and expenditure is logged when it is still fresh in your mind and receipts are to hand.

Many people choose to set up their accounts on a personal computer and there are many suitable computer software programs available. However, if you prefer to have handwritten accounts these too are perfectly acceptable and an accounts book with pre-printed columns can be bought from many high street stores. Accounts books can also be purchased from the National Childminding Association and these are straightforward and easy to understand.

◆ **TIP** ◆

Your accounts should be neat and accurate so that you can see, at a glance, what you have earned, what you have spent and any profit or loss you have made.

HOW TO KEEP YOUR ACCOUNTS

The example shown on page 98 is one way of setting out income and expenditure. The trick is to find a method that works for you and to be disciplined when completing your accounts. Set aside some time, say once a week or once a month, when you can devote yourself to getting your accounts up to date. By being organised you will save yourself a lot of hassle in the long run.

Make sure you keep all your receipts and number these. You can then write the number of the receipt next to the item it relates to on your account sheet so that you can see easily which receipt matches which expense. It is a good idea to either staple the receipts to the appropriate page of your accounts or keep them in numerical order in a separate folder.

As I have mentioned before the way you set out your accounts is entirely up to you. Look for a method of recording your earnings and expenses which works for you and which you find easy to use.

Here is an example of what your income and expenditure sheets might look like:

Week commencing 7 February 200X

INCOME   EXPENDITURE

DATE	ITEM	AMOUNT	DATE	ITEM	AMOUNT
07/02/0X	Fees – David Sam	75.00 25.00	07/02/0X	Food for children's teas	6.35
14/02/0X	Fees – Cathy	15.00	14/02/0X	Paper Paint Glitter	4.99 6.50 .99
21/02/0X	Fees – Cathy Sam	15.00 25.00	21/02/0X	Petrol	25.00
28/02/0X	Fees – Cathy Milk refund	15.00 13.75	28/02/0X	Postage to NCMA Toilet rolls Professional carpet clean	.28 4.99 25.00

By adding up the figures in each of the columns headed amount you will be able to see, at a glance, how much money you have received for the month and how much money you have spent.

If you choose to set up your own accounts system, it is important that you are accurate and that you are aware of the items which the Inland Revenue will allow you to set against your tax liability.

START-UP COSTS

These costs vary from one childminder to another and will depend on factors such as the age and number of children you are registered to care for. Start-up costs might include items such as:

◆ toys, books and games;

◆ safety equipment such as safety gates, smoke alarms, fire guards, fire extinguishers and fire blankets;

◆ insurance;

◆ advertising.

If you are eligible for a start-up grant you will not be expected to pay tax on it. However, it is important that you are aware that you will not be able to offset the items you have purchased from your grant against your personal tax.

EXPENSES

Any *reasonable* expenses are allowed in full. You will not be required to produce a receipt for items under £10 but if you purchase one or several items together costing more than £10 then you must keep your receipts.

Below is a list of items which are widely regarded as reasonable general expenses for which you are allowed to deduct the full cost:

◆ food and drinks including milk, fruit, biscuits, crisps etc;

◆ toys and equipment for play provision such as paper, paint, crayons, collage materials etc;

◆ baby requisites such as nappies, baby wipes, cotton wool, nappy liners, bibs etc;

◆ towels, face cloths and soap;

◆ toilet paper and tissues;

◆ kitchen roll and paper towels;

◆ soap powder;

◆ washing up liquid;

◆ cleaning equipment such as disinfectant, air freshener, toilet cleaner;

◆ bin liners;

◆ dish cloths, floor cloths and mops;

◆ disposable gloves and aprons;

◆ first aid kit and the contents including: bandages, micropore, dressings, scissors, thermometer etc;

◆ equipment (the provision, maintenance and replacement costs) of items such as cot, pushchair, high chair, booster seat and car seat, bed linen and sterilising equipment;

◆ safety equipment (the provision, maintenance and replacement costs) of items such as fireguard, cupboard locks, fences and gates, glass protection etc.

◆ telephone calls and postage – you may need to write to or telephone the parents of the children you care for or perhaps organisations such as the National Childminding Association or Ofsted.

In addition to the expenses incurred *directly* through your work as a childminder you are also entitled to certain other 'allowable' expenses such as heating and lighting, water rates, council tax and wear and tear on your home and contents. The percentage you can claim will depend on the number of hours you work as a childminder and the table below shows this in more detail.

Hours worked	Wear and tear	Council tax	Heat and light	Water rates
Full time (40 hours/week)	10%	10%	33% of costs	10%
Part time (20 hours/week)	10%	5%	17% of costs	5%
Between full and part (30 hours/week)	10%	7%	25% of costs	7%

The expenses are calculated according to the number of hours you *actually* work and not the number of hours you are being paid for by each parent. For example, if you care for one child for eight hours per day for five days per week you will be working a 40-hour week entitling you to the full-time deduction in allowable expenses. However if you are caring for two children for four hours per day for five days per week you will be working 20 hours per week but getting paid for 40 hours. However you will only be entitled to claim the part-time deduction of allowable expenses.

We will now look at each of the following categories in the above chart in closer detail.

Wear and tear

You will be allowed to claim one tenth of your childminding income to cover 'wear and tear' on items in your home which are not classed as being for the exclusive use of your childminding business, such as carpets and furniture. However, this deduction means you will not be able to claim tax relief for the actual cost of these items as and when they need replacing. You can, however, claim the cost of cleaning household items, such as carpets and loose covers separately, providing these costs are deemed reasonable and the need for cleaning is actually down to your childminding activities.

Council tax

Council tax can be claimed as a work-related expense. The amount of council tax you can claim depends on the number of hours you work – from 10 per cent for full-time childminding hours to 5 per cent for part-time hours.

Heat and light

To claim a proportion of your heating and lighting costs you must remember to keep your fuel bills. It is possible for you to claim a third of your total household fuel bills if you work as a childminder on a full-time basis. Scaled down proportions are allowed for childminders working fewer than 40 hours per week.

Water rates

If you are working 40 hours or more per week you are entitled to claim one tenth of the cost of your water rates or water meter charges. Once again a proportionate amount, as shown in the previous chart, can be claimed for part-time childminding hours.

In addition to the above four categories it is possible to claim for further expenses such as:

Rent

Although you will not be able to deduct a percentage of your mortgage repayments it is possible for rent payers to deduct one tenth of the amount they pay in rent.

Free milk

As mentioned in Chapter 1, you are entitled to claim the cost of one third of a pint of milk for each child, under the age of five years, that you care for. You can request the appropriate form from the Welfare Food Reimbursement Unit by contacting them on 0870 720 3063.

TAX FOR THE SELF EMPLOYED

As a self-employed person *you* are responsible for keeping accurate accounts and business records and for paying any income tax that you may owe. You will be expected to complete your own tax records and will be known as being 'self-assessed'. We looked at ways of keeping accounts earlier in this chapter and it is important to remember that the figures you enter on your tax return *must* coincide with the figures entered in your accounts. This is the way in which you can prove to your tax office whether or not you will be liable to pay tax.

Personal tax allowance

You will be entitled to earn a certain amount of money, known as your personal tax allowance, before you will be expected to pay tax. Your personal tax allowance will be calculated depending on your own personal circumstances. If your income is higher than your personal allowance then you have a legal obligation to complete and submit a self-assessment form to the Inland Revenue. If you receive a self-assessment form it does not necessarily mean that you will have to pay tax. However, failure to submit the form, when requested, could result in a fine from the Inland Revenue.

Many childminders find that they do not earn sufficient money from their childminding business alone to make them liable to pay tax. The amount of tax you will have to pay will depend on the amount of money you have earned, after expenses have been deducted. Expenses can be high for a childminder who has a number of children to care for. In addition to everyday expenses you will also be regularly buying consumables such as paper, paints and play equipment. The cost of all these items can be offset against your tax resulting in your net income being reduced. If you have other sources of income, however, such as a second job, savings or a pension then the income on these must also be taken into account and will of course increase your net income making it possible that you may need to pay income tax.

MAKING A PROFIT OR A LOSS?

Although the amount you charge has to be competitive it must also reflect the service you provide and cover the costs that you incur. There is no doubt that if you substantially undercut all your competitors your business may be full, but working for a minimum amount of money is not what you should be aiming for. No childminder who has three full-time vacancies will be happy limping along caring for one child part time.

If you have had your premises rigorously inspected, gone through the registration process and gained the necessary training and qualifications to become a childminder, you obviously want your business to be a success and your places to be full. However, you must still look at the business side of childminding and put things into perspective. Drastically reducing your fees, to secure custom, will not make your business a success. In fact quite the reverse may be true. If you are not covering your overheads you may be looking after three full-time children but, after feeding them and providing resources and equipment, it is possible that you could end up with your business making a loss!

◆ TIP ◆

You must be realistic when setting your fees.

The fees you set and the number of children you are registered to care for will have a significant impact on the amount of money you earn. The fees you collect, less all your costs, will result in one of the following three outcomes.

Making a profit

This is obviously the best position to be in. Any money you make, after all costs and wages have been deducted, is seen as a profit and this money can be reinvested in your business. You may like to use the money to purchase further toys and equipment, replace old items or extend your own knowledge through a training course. It is healthy for your business to make a profit, and you should be aiming for this at all times. If you choose to use your profit for personal use you must remember that this will be subject to income tax and national insurance, like your wage.

Breaking even

This means that the fees you receive will match exactly the expenses you have incurred, including wages. You will not have made any surplus money nor will your accounts show a loss. Providing you are happy with the amount of wages you are earning this is not a bad position to be in. However you must remember that if you are not making a profit, you will be unable to make improvements to your business or invest in new toys and equipment unless you do so with your own money. This will result in your business effectively making a loss.

Making a loss

This means that the amount of fees you receive are less than the costs you have incurred. If your overheads exceed your income and your business is making a loss you will need to find extra money from elsewhere in order for your business to keep afloat. This is not a good position to be in and if you find yourself making a loss you will need to reassess your situation immediately and work out a plan to get your business back on track.

WHAT CAN I DO IF MY BUSINESS IS MAKING A LOSS?

There may be several reasons why a business is making a loss. Perhaps to begin with, when you have just set up your business and have incorporated costs for equipment, toys, insurance and registration fees, you may find yourself out of pocket for some time until you have built up a reputation and successfully filled your vacancies. This is to be expected. You can not realistically expect all your vacancies to be filled within a couple of days of having your registration granted. However there are several ways in which you can drum up business and we looked at these in Chapter 5.

In addition to waiting for your business to take off and word to get around you may find yourself making a loss through one of a number of reasons.

- A child may leave your setting suddenly and you have not had a chance to advertise the vacancy.

- A child may leave your setting having moved house or school and you are unable to fill the vacancy despite having a notice period.

- A parent may be on maternity leave and, although you agreed to a reduction in fees during this period, you find that this is not working for you, from a business point of view.

- You may have agreed to a reduction in fees because of caring for a school teacher's child or a child whose parents are separated and take their child away from your setting for a large number of weeks per annum.

There are a great many reasons why your vacancies may not be full, and therefore your earning potential is reduced, and you must look at each one separately.

Extended absence

If your business is in trouble due to something that you have agreed with the parents beforehand, for example, a large number of weeks absent from the setting due to holidays or maternity leave then you must assess the situation and discuss your concerns with the parents.

◆ TIP ◆

It is *so* important to think carefully before offering or agreeing to reductions and concessions. It is often not until much later, when reality takes hold, that you realise just how much reduced rates can affect your business.

You may genuinely want to help the parents out and not wish to risk losing their custom but, if the arrangement results in your business making a loss, you will not be helping anyone if you go out of business and they and the other children you care for will have to find alternative childcare.

I have found that, although discussing money matters is something that not many people relish, when it comes down to it most parents are very reasonable and, if you explain your predicament, a compromise can usually be found. Perhaps they may agree to pay a higher retainer fee or bring their child for some of the weeks. No one should reasonably expect you to work long hours and end up making a loss. Point out to parents that you are only allowed to care for a certain number of children under the conditions of your registration, and if one or more of the children on your books are away from the setting for a lengthy period of time this can have a devastating effect on your finances.

Maternity leave
In the case of a parent taking maternity leave this can, depending on the amount of money you are losing, often be managed. The maternity leave is usually only for a six-month period and when the child returns it is to be expected that their sibling will also be in attendance and the money you have lost during the maternity period can be quickly recuperated when caring for two children.

Whatever the situation, you should not be expected to subsidise your business, on a regular basis, with your own savings or at the expense of your weekly wage.

◆ TIP ◆

No business can be classed as a success if the person running it is not entitled to draw a reasonable amount of money for the work they do.

If you find yourself having agreed to lengthy absences, and your business can not withstand this reduction in fees, then you must speak to the parents as soon as possible and come to an agreement. Unlike maternity leave, if you have allowed parents to only bring their children to you during school term time – and they pay for this service during those weeks only – then you will need to be able to bear the loss amounting to approximately thirteen weeks' fees *every* year. In my experience this can only work if you have other children who require your services during these weeks and the places can therefore be kept filled.

◆ TIP ◆

Don't be afraid to set your fees at an amount which means that you are making a profit. This is a healthy position to be in and will ultimately benefit the children you care for as you will have the funds to reinvest in your business, to make improvements or buy new toys and equipment.

Turning things round

If you find that your business is making a loss it is important that you acknowledge your finances and act upon them quickly in order to avoid going out of business.

There are three things you can do to change the position.

1. **Increase the number of children you are currently caring for.** You could employ an assistant so that the number of children you are registered to care for can be increased. Remember, though, that you will have staff wages to pay along with additional tax and national insurance contributions and this may well mean that the profit you actually earn from looking after more children will not necessarily be very much.

If you are happy with the number of children you are registered to care for, and the loss you are making is simply because you have vacancies, you must think about ways of advertising your business. It does not cost very much to produce and display posters and by speaking to your local school, nursery and playgroup you may be able to generate business. Always let people know about your work.

◆ TIP ◆

Word of mouth is a great way of getting business and if the person you are speaking to doesn't need your services they may know someone who does!

---

2. **Increase your fees**. Make sure that you are complying with your contract before introducing any increases in fees. You must give plenty of notice of your intention to increase the charges you make; ideally a price increase should take place on the review date of the contract. Explain to the parents why you need to charge more for your service.

3. **Reduce your costs**. Some of the costs incurred by childminders are essential, such as public liability insurance, and therefore these *must* be paid. However, you may be able to decrease the amount of money you spend in other areas. It is essential however that any reductions you make in the amount of money you spend does not affect the quality of service you provide.

◆ TIP ◆

If you need to increase your fees, explain your reasons to the parents and give them plenty of notice beforehand. Don't be apologetic when setting your fees and don't feel obliged to reduce the amount you charge just to secure business. Most parents are willing to pay a competitive fee for good quality, reliable childcare.

8

Everyday Running of Your Childminding Business

PLANNING

In order for your business to run smoothly and efficiently it is important that you spend time planning. Some of your days will be repetitive, and you will have routines which you will have to follow time and time again, such as taking children to school or playgroup. You must organise your time effectively so that the children you are taking to school get there on time and that you are never late to collect them at the end of the school day.

Your day as a childminder is likely to start early and finish late, as you will be expected to fit in around the working hours of the parents whose children you are caring for. It is important that you are ready to start your day at the time you have agreed on your contract.

◆ TIP ◆

You are a professional person running a business from home and you must show this professionalism at all times.

If your contracted hours are 7.30am then you must be ready to receive children, and begin working, at this time.

The busiest times of your working day are likely to be during the arrival and departure of the children to your setting. You may have several parents dropping their children off simultaneously and you must make sure that you are organised sufficiently in order that you create opportunities for the parents to communicate any important information with you, when necessary. It is difficult to give your undivided attention to a parent if their child is jumping up and down in front of you trying to tell you an exciting story about what they have done that weekend. However, if you prepare yourself for this hectic time, and have a suitable activity ready for the child on arrival, it will give you the vital couple of minutes needed to communicate with the parent before they leave your setting.

DAILY ROUTINES

There will be important times in your childminding day which you must be aware of, and you must plan your day around these times appropriately. Things to consider are:

◆ the arrival and departure of the children and their parents to your setting;

◆ times you have to take children to and collect them from playgroup, nursery and school;

◆ times for snacks and meals;

◆ feed times for babies;

◆ naps and rests;

◆ domestic activities;

◆ visits and outings;

◆ indoor play;

◆ outdoor play;

◆ toilet training.

Being on time
If you have parents who drop their children off near to the times that you need to leave home on your journey to school or nursery, it is important that they are made aware of your routine and ensure that they

are not late as this may put your whole routine in jeopardy. They may have a six-month-old child and not realise the school start times, so you need to make them aware of the latest time they can drop their child off with you, allowing you plenty of time for your journey to school without rushing or compromising the safety of any of the children in your care.

If you agree to provide a school drop off and collection service you must ensure that you do this on time every day. There is no excuse for the children to be late to school unless in very extreme circumstances. It is not acceptable to take a child to school late simply because you have not organised your morning appropriately.

◆ TIP ◆

Prepare yourself in advance for journeys to school and nursery. Make sure everyone's coats and shoes are to hand and that the pushchair, if you are using one, is ready to use with the safety harness fitted.

Mealtimes should be kept as much to a routine as possible. They should be enjoyable times for everyone and should not be rushed. It is important that you try to create a relaxed atmosphere and make mealtimes social occasions. The times you choose for meals should be arranged according to the times the children start their day with you and they must fit in with your normal day-to-day routines of school runs, naps and play times.

The chart on page 112 shows a typical childminder's daily routine. It can be adapted to suit each individual childminder's circumstances.

Young babies

Obviously your daily routine will differ if you care for a young baby who needs to be bottle fed every three to four hours, and you will need to make sure that the baby's feeds fit in around other routines which you may have. It is important that you plan the baby's feeds in agreement with the parent so that neither the child goes hungry nor do you turn up late to collect children from school.

Time	Activity or planned routine.
7.30 am	Arrival of children.
8.00 am	Breakfast.
8.45 am	Set off on journey to school.
9.00 am	Drop children off at school.
9.10 am	Arrive back home from school. Morning play activities.
10.00 am	Snack.
10.15 am	Outdoor play.
11.00 am	Visit to local library.
11.45 am	Prepare lunch.
12.00 pm	Lunch.
12.45 pm	Set off on journey to nursery.
1.00 pm	Drop child off at nursery.
1.10 pm	Arrive back home from nursery. Nap time and quiet activities.
2.30 pm	Play activities.
3.15 pm	Set off on journey to collect from nursery and school.
3.30 pm	Collect child from nursery.
3.35 pm	Collect children from school.
3.50 pm	Arrive back home from school and nursery.
4.00 pm	Tea or snack and drink.
4.15 pm	Afternoon activities, time for homework, etc.
5.45 pm	Start to tidy toys away and visit the toilet in time to go home.
5.50 pm	Parents start to arrive to collect children.
6.00 pm	Last child leaves setting after chat with parent about their day.

Going to clubs and activities

In addition to taking and collecting children from playgroup, nursery or school, you may also be asked to take school-aged children to various clubs and classes such as dancing class, gym club, swimming club, language or music lessons and you should consider very carefully whether this is something you can accommodate. Remember that taking and collecting from lots of schools and clubs can be very tiring and time consuming and it is not always something that younger children appreciate having to do. You must also bear in mind the times that parents collect their children from your setting and ensure that you are back at home in time for this.

Getting ready to go out

Apart from the actual travelling time needed to take and collect children from a variety of schools and clubs you must also bear in mind how much time is needed to get yourself and the children ready. You will need to ensure that everyone has waterproof clothing available when necessary or sun cream and hats in hot weather. You need to make sure you have ample time for safety procedures such as strapping children into the car or buggy and making sure that children have visited the toilet prior to setting off. You will need to anticipate how long your journey will take and make time for unexpected delays such as heavy traffic.

◆ TIP ◆

It is essential that you are good at planning ahead and practice good time keeping at all times.

Changing routines

You must adjust and change your routines as and when the children in your care grow and develop. A child's sleep patterns will change as they grow from being a baby into a toddler and the need for frequent toilet routines will be necessary when a child is beginning to start potty training. Any changes to the usual routines will need to be discussed and agreed with the parents so that you can adapt your times to fit in with the families of the children you care for as much as possible. Obviously if you care for several children it will probably be necessary for a certain element of flexibility to be introduced and all this should be discussed with the parents.

Meeting parents' wishes

You must try, whenever possible, to meet the parents' wishes. A parent may request that their child does not have a long nap during the day so they can get off to sleep easier in the evening, giving the parents time to themselves. Alternatively, a parent may request that their child does have a long sleep in the afternoon so that they can spend time with them in the evening. You must, whenever possible, adhere to these wishes. Of course, no one can be expected to make a child go to sleep if they are not tired and likewise you should not be expected to refuse a tired child the opportunity of rest. If you are finding it impossible to carry out parental wishes then you must notify them immediately in order for a compromise to be found.

Spontaneous play

One of the luxuries of being self employed is that you can often decide what you do and when you do it. After you have dealt with the necessary routines, you will be left with parts of your day when you can choose the activities or outings you wish to take part in. There should always be room in your day for 'spontaneous' play; for example if a beautiful summer's day clouds over and there is a sudden shower, try to find the time to pull on waterproofs and take the children splashing in puddles and looking at rainbows. Going for walks should be part of your routine in all weathers and, providing the children have suitable clothing, these walks should be enjoyable. It is important that children are allowed to explore their immediate environment during unhurried walks. Trips to the park, walks in the snow and kicking up the leaves in autumn all provide interesting learning opportunities.

Domestic chores

Working with children at home will provide you with certain opportunities to carry out domestic chores. Many parents choose childminders over a nursery setting because they like the idea of their child spending time in a home-based setting doing the sort of things they would probably have been doing if they were at home with their parents.

That is not to say that parents would be forgiving if they discovered that you had taken their children on a monthly shopping spree at the supermarket or stuck them in front of the television for hours whilst you did a mountain of ironing or a spring clean of the house. These types of domestic activities should *never* be undertaken whilst you are caring for someone else's children.

♦ TIP ♦

You are providing a professional service and as such must ensure that whatever activities you do have a beneficial effect on the children in your care.

A trip to the shops to purchase a small number of items or for the children to choose a birthday present for someone special will be beneficial. Unlike a tiring supermarket shop, these purchases can be done at a time when the stores are quiet and it can be an excellent source for learning.

Learning through participation

Try letting the children choose which birthday card to buy. Talk to them about the things you are purchasing and why. Encourage them to pay for the goods with the money you give them. Older children can count out the coins and try to work out how much change they should receive.

Domestic activities such as setting the table, weighing and preparing food, watering plants etc are all necessary everyday activities which can be beneficial to children's learning if they are allowed to take part.

It is very important, when planning your daily routines, to be realistic about the length of time needed to carry out certain activities. Setting the table and clearing away after a meal may take you a couple of minutes if you are doing it yourself, but if you allow the children to help it can increase to 15 minutes. When you allow the children to help with the domestic activities it is important not to rush them or have unrealistic expectations of their achievements. Children will flourish in a relaxed atmosphere and will learn if given the time and opportunity.

FOOD AND DRINK

It is important to plan and provide healthy snacks and meals for the children you are caring for. You must take into account the preferences of the children and any cultural or dietary requirements. Try to plan your meals in advance so that you can ensure that you have sufficient ingredients to prepare the meal you are intending to make. Food should be presented attractively and children should be encouraged to try a variety of different foods. You should be aware of the factors which may affect a child's appetite and know how to deal with them. For example a child may not be interested in food if they are:

- tired;
- feeling unwell;
- excited;
- absorbed in an activity;
- feeling emotional or stressed.

It is important that you recognise any symptoms of a poor appetite and report any concerns you may have to the child's parent.

You can encourage good eating habits by:

- **Encouraging the children to take part** in choosing and preparing meals and helping to set the table.

- **Providing healthy food** such as fresh fruit and vegetables.

- **Providing healthy snacks** such as fruit, carrot sticks, celery, raisins etc instead of sweets and biscuits.

- **Introducing new foods gradually.** If a child appears to dislike a particular food, wait a while and then reintroduce it at a later date.

◆ **Offering small portions** with the option of a further helping rather than overfilling a plate and putting the child off.

◆ **Presenting the food** attractively.

◆ **Giving children the opportunity** of different eating experiences such as picnics, restaurants etc.

◆ **Avoiding using food as a bribe,** and never withholding food as a punishment.

◆ **Making mealtimes enjoyable,** social occasions.

Menus

Below is an example of a weekly menu, showing meals which could be adapted to suit your childminding practice.

Meal/snack	Monday	Tuesday	Wednesday	Thursday	Friday
Breakfast at 8.00am	Weetabix with milk	Porridge with milk	Rice Krispies with milk	Weetabix with milk	Porridge with milk
Snack at 10.30am	Milkshake and fruit	Fresh fruit juice and a biscuit	Milkshake and fruit	Fresh fruit juice and a piece of cake	Milkshake and fruit
Lunch at 12.15pm	Shepherds pie and vegetables and gravy. Rice pudding	Steamed fish in parsley sauce, mashed potato and vegetables. Fresh fruit salad	Roast beef and Yorkshire pudding with new potatoes and vegetables. Lemon meringue pie	Chicken and vegetable casserole. Apple pie and custard.	Meat and potato pie with fresh seasonal vegetables. Rhubarb crumble and custard
Snack at 3.00pm	Drink and a biscuit	Milkshake and fruit	Drink and a fruit scone	Milkshake and fruit	Drink and a biscuit
Tea at 4.30pm	Sandwiches, crisps, fruit, yoghurt, cake and drink	Scrambled egg on toast, yoghurt and drink	Vegetable broth and wholemeal bread, fromage frais and drink	Sandwiches, crisps, fruit, yoghurt, biscuit and drink	Boiled egg with soldiers, fresh fruit, biscuit and drink

It is important to liaise with parents at all times with regard to their attitude towards certain foods, in particular sweets, biscuits and fizzy drinks.

KEEPING DIARIES

It is vitally important that you share information, on a daily basis, with the parents of the children you care for. Because of the hectic schedules of many parents, and the fact that you may have two or more parents collecting children from your setting at the same time, it can often be difficult to get the chance to speak, confidentially, to parents, and I recommend the use of a 'daily diary' for this reason. The diary, which goes back and forth from your setting to the child's home, can be used to note down any important information you feel it is necessary to share with the parents, such as:

◆ how the child has been spending their time with you
◆ what they have achieved
◆ meals they have eaten that day
◆ any concerns.

If you are caring for a baby or young child who cannot yet talk, the diary is an invaluable source of communication between yourself and the child's parents. You should note down the baby's:

◆ feed patterns
◆ nappy changes
◆ sleep.

Important information such as forthcoming holidays and contract renewal dates can also be logged in the diary. If you have any worries or concerns it can be helpful to note these in the diary with a request for the parent to telephone you, perhaps later that evening, when you both have the time to discuss the matter privately, in further detail.

A diary, although an extremely helpful tool, should not be used instead of verbal communication. It is a way of sharing information with a parent but it must never take the place of regular face-to-face discussions. It could be that in some cases you rarely see the parents of a child in your care, perhaps because they are older school-aged children and are dropped off at the gate in the morning or are brought and collected by a relative. If this is the case I would advise you to arrange a mutually convenient time, perhaps once a month or more if necessary, to meet with the parents or telephone them to share information or concerns. Never wait for a problem to get out of hand before tackling it. Often by dealing with a situation early on you can avoid any unnecessary problems later.

◆ TIP ◆

I recommend that, in addition to the daily diary for parents, you equip each child with their own special book and folder. A scrapbook with the child's name and picture on the front is an ideal way of storing paintings and drawings and is a wonderful keepsake for years to come. A small plastic folder is a good way of keeping the child's work together before they take it home.

HOW TO WRITE AND MAINTAIN APPROPRIATE POLICIES

As a self-employed person running your own business from home it is important to remember that, although you are providing a service, your house is still your home and as such should be treated with respect.

You will need to decide, prior to any child entering your setting, what your boundaries are going to be and how you are going to implement them. It is a good idea to think carefully about your aims and goals and write a policy to reflect these. Any policy you draw up should be displayed on the walls of your setting and a copy of each policy should be given to the parents of the child before a placement commences.

The main areas I would suggest policies for are:

Behaviour
Most parents accept the need for children to have boundaries when it comes to behaviour; however it is important to realise that not all parents will share your views when it comes to discipline. You can usually determine early on whether or not a set of parents share your own views and values and this is one of the reasons why it is important

to discuss things such as behaviour at the initial interview. You should be able to tell at this stage whether or not you feel able to work with the parents or whether you feel there would be too many conflicting opinions for you to offer suitable childcare.

This is another reason why I would never advise you to sign a contract on the first meeting – always try to allow yourself time to think and reflect on the interview and mull over the points and issues raised. When the time comes for the signing of contracts I would advise you to, once again, go over any policies you have and allow parents to ask any questions.

Confidentiality

It is very important that you respect confidentiality at all times. You may be caring for children whose respective parents are friends or, worse still, enemies, and they may at times try to glean information from you about the other family's circumstances. You must *never* partake in gossip or divulge any information about other families of the children you care for.

Equal opportunities

You must be aware of how you can promote equal opportunities by treating all the children, and their parents and families, as individuals and with equal concern. You must respect each family, their culture, beliefs and religion, and you must know how to discourage prejudice and stereotypical attitudes within your setting. It is important that you are confident at tackling discrimination and prejudicial remarks.

◆ TIP ◆

Think about how you would tackle a parent who showed discriminatory behaviour in your setting. Would you know how to respond if they made an offensive remark about another child you were caring for?

In addition to the above policies you should also set out an emergency plan showing details of the procedure to be followed in the event of an emergency and give a copy of this plan to the parents of the children in your care.

Example policies

Below are examples of the policies you could use. They can be adapted to suit your own requirements.

BEHAVIOUR POLICY

To enable all children to enjoy their time with me I have a few requests that I would appreciate your help in achieving.

PLEASE say 'Excuse me' if you would like to pass by.
PLEASE sit down on the chairs and do not jump on the furniture.
PLEASE walk around the toys so that they do not get broken.
PLEASE be kind and gentle and treat others as you would like to be treated.
PLEASE try to share and take turns.
PLEASE take muddy shoes off at the door.
PLEASE help each other to get things done.
PLEASE be honest and tell the truth.

PLEASE REMEMBER we are all different, we have different ideas and ways of doing things and that is what makes us all special.

NO-ONE IS PERFECT!

The things that you put in your own Behaviour Policy should reflect the views you have on what is or is not acceptable to *you* in *your* home. It is a good idea to talk through the way you expect children to behave, whilst they are in your care, with the child's parents. They may have completely different ideas of what constitutes acceptable behaviour and this is something that must be cleared up early on. The children may be allowed to roam their own home in muddy shoes and eat their lunch in front of the television but, if this is something that you object to, you must make your own rules clear and ask that parents help you to implement them when they are bringing and collecting their children.

The times when parents are in your home with their child are often the times when things will start to become unravelled. Children learn, from very early on, what they can and cannot get away with and which adult is the soft touch. Often parents who are collecting their children after a long day at work will indulge them out of tiredness or feelings of guilt but, if their child is using your sofa as a trampoline just because their parent is present and they know this is something you have asked them not to do, then don't be afraid of telling them to get down. *Never* allow the child to do something when their parent is present that you would not allow them to do if they weren't. It is confusing to the child and undermines your authority in your own home.

◆ TIP ◆

Your rules should still apply whether a parent is present in your setting or not. Do not allow a child to undermine your authority when their mum or dad is in your setting. Let parents and children know that you expect them to treat your home with respect!

CONFIDENTIALITY POLICY

Maintaining confidentiality is a central part of working as a professional childminder. You will appreciate that, as a childminder, I will acquire a lot of information and knowledge about the children that I care for, and their families.

A lot of the information I am told is of a sensitive nature and you can be assured that I will do everything possible in order to keep this information confidential at all times.

I will endeavour not to pass on any information, without your prior permission (except in very extreme circumstances when it may be in the interest of the child to do so), to any individual.

Please help me to maintain confidentiality by refraining from asking me for any information relating to another child in my care.

Please remember that *everyone* has the right to confidentiality and your help in maintaining this within my setting is much appreciated.

It is often difficult to know what to say to someone who is asking you questions about a child you care for. Although you do not wish to be rude neither must you breach your confidentiality policy. Politely tell the person that you are not at liberty to divulge information about the children or the families that you care for.

EQUAL OPPORTUNITIES POLICY

Regardless of their racial origins, cultural background, gender, age, family grouping or disability *all* children in my care will be:

Treated as individuals and with equal concern.
Treated fairly and equally.
Given the opportunity to develop and learn.
Encouraged to learn about people different from themselves and to respect and enjoy those differences.

I intend to promote, at all times:
Respect of others, their culture, beliefs and religion.

I intend to discourage at all times:
Stereotypical attitudes.
Prejudice of any nature.
Negative images.

I will not tolerate, at any time:
Discrimination towards any child because of their skin colour, gender, cultural or family background, racial origins or disability.

**YOUR ASSISTANCE IN HELPING TO PROMOTE
THIS POLICY IS GREATLY APPRECIATED**

It is important, whilst ensuring that parents are aware of what you will and will not tolerate from children whilst they are on your premises, that you also make sure your expectations are realistic and that your methods for achieving your aims and goals are effective and take into account each child's age and understanding. You must realise that no two families are alike and therefore not everyone will be in complete agreement with you.

There are many different forms of parenting and no one can reasonably say that their methods are right whilst others are wrong.

◆ **TIP** ◆

As a childminder you must learn to understand, accept and tolerate a wide range of parenting ideas.

If a parent does not agree with the boundaries and policies you have set, it is important to discuss any concerns they may have prior to signing the contract and try to compromise whenever possible.

If you feel it is necessary to revise or update your policies once you have been childminding for some time, then you must draw up a new policy, give a copy to the parents of the children and discuss any changes with them to ensure that everyone is aware of the changes and why you feel it is necessary to make them.

PARENTAL PERMISSION

It is important that you obtain *written* parental permission for various procedures you may like to carry out within your setting. These procedures might include:

◆ taking a child on an outing;
◆ taking photographs of the children in your care;
◆ videoing an event the children are taking part in, such as a concert or birthday party;
◆ transporting a child in a car;
◆ seeking medical advice when necessary.

Suitable forms seeking permission for the above can be obtained from the National Childminding Association or you could devise your own forms and get the parents to sign them.

EQUIPMENT CHECKS

It is important to be aware of how to continually check the toys and equipment you are using. Toys and equipment which are in constant use by several children will become broken and worn.

Checking toys

You should get into the habit of checking your toys daily; either when you get them out for the children to play with or at the end of the day when the children have gone home and you are tidying things away. I would recommend that toys are sorted and stored in suitable boxes so that you can see at a glance which toys are kept where. This is a good way of ensuring that the correct toys are given to the correct children. For example a box which contains toys suitable for babies such as rattles, soft toys etc, should not contain anything with small parts which could pose a threat to the child's safety. By storing your construction toys together, your puzzles and games together and your dressing up and role play items together you can immediately find the correct toys to suit the needs of the children you are caring for and won't have to rummage through endless boxes removing unsuitable items.

Checking equipment

In addition to checking toys you should set aside some time, say once a month, when you can spend quality time carefully checking each item of equipment for wear and tear. You should make a note in your diary when the time is approaching for an equipment check and then devise a plan similar to the one below to record your findings. As well as the equipment you use indoors you should also check your pushchairs and outdoor apparatus such as swings, slides etc. These items of play equipment must be checked after the winter months, when they have perhaps been used very little and adverse weather conditions could have affected their safety and suitability.

Below is an example of an equipment check chart.

Date of check	Item	Findings	Repaired/replaced
14 February 200X	Constructions toys	3 toys with broken parts	Replaced
14 February 200X	Highchair	Frayed reins	Replaced
14 February 200X	Changing mat	Split in plastic covering	Replaced
14 February 200X	Outdoor climbing frame	Screw loose by ladder	Repaired
14 February 200X	Motor vehicles	Missing tyre on tractor	Replaced

FIRE DRILLS

It is important to carry out regular fire drills. Fire drills should be practised with the children so that they are aware of what is expected of them in the case of a fire. Children who are old enough should be taught an effective method of evacuating the house and they should realise the importance of remaining calm and doing exactly as they are told.

It is a good idea to make a chart for your fire drills similar to the one below and make a note in your diary, say once a month, to practice the drill. You should change the days and times that you practice the drill frequently in order that *all* children get the chance to practice. It is pointless doing your fire drill every Monday if you have several children who only attend your setting on Thursday and Friday.

Date	Time	No of children	Effectiveness of drill/ improvements necessary	Next drill
Fri 10/2/0X	11.15am	1 – age 3 1 – age 6 months	Very effective – older child understood and carried out requests calmly.	Mon 13/03/0X
Mon 13/3/0X	2.30pm	2 – age 2	Took a little longer than I would have liked to get the children out of the building. Decided to practice the drill again next week with these particular children.	Mon 20/03/0X

OBSERVATIONS AND ASSESSMENTS

Part of your daily routine should include observing and assessing children. Often you will be doing this without realising it. As you spend time with the children you will notice their abilities changing and improving. A baby will learn how to roll over, sit up supported, sit independently, start to crawl, learn to walk etc. These natural progressions are expected and are often taken for granted.

Observing and assessing children is an important part of a childminder's job, not only to ensure that a child is progressing at an adequate rate, but to determine what areas, if any, a child may need extra encouragement and support in and whether or not there are any areas for concern. It is very difficult to determine at what age a child should be crawling or walking as no two children are alike and each child develops at his or her own pace. Whilst one child may crawl at six months another may never crawl but progress straight to standing and walking. When carrying out observations and assessments, we take into account the 'average' child's progression and try to base our findings on these.

Observing children is an important part of planning. By watching and observing the children you care for you can:

- **Learn about the child's needs** – what their strengths and weaknesses are. Your findings may be useful if it is decided that a child needs specialist help.

- **Provide records for parents**. Parents will often ask about their child's progress and by observing and assessing the children you will be able to supply the parents with accurate information.

- **Check on development and growth**. The observations and assessments you carry out will enable you to ascertain if there are any problems with a child's development and growth.

- **Plan activities**. Using your observations and assessments is an excellent way of planning your activities effectively to ensure that they are appropriate for the children.

Observing a child is not as easy as it sounds. Although it involves watching the child, you must be aware of the things to look out for. For example, which hand a child uses the most when carrying out a particular task, whether their movements are awkward or co-ordinated, fast or slow, whether they enjoyed the task, found it easy or difficult, whether they preferred to stand, sit or crouch to carry out the activity.

There are many different ways to observe and assess a child. They include the following:

Written observations

This is when you note down what a child is doing during a short period of time.

Checklists and tick charts

This is when you use a standard chart to record a child's aspect of development. The chart may ask questions such as:

1. Can the child count to 10?
2. Does the child recognise the basic colours?
3. Does the child recognise the letters in the alphabet?
4. Can the child throw and catch a ball?

Tapes and videos

It is essential that you obtain written parental permission prior to recording any child. Tapes and videos can be a useful method of observing children, providing they are not aware of what you are doing otherwise they may play up for the camera.

The way you observe and assess the children in your care will be entirely up to you, but you *must* always seek parental permission prior to carrying out an observation or assessment. You may feel that you are unsure of what and how to assess, and if this is the case then an appropriate course would be beneficial to you. Your local authority should be able to advise you of the availability of a suitable short course in your area.

SUPPORT GROUPS AND LOCAL COMMUNITY RESOURCES

Support groups

Local groups have been set up in many areas by childminders. These groups enable childminders to get together socially, often on a weekly basis, and they are a means of providing support and advice. As I have said before, childminding can be a lonely profession and support groups can offer an opportunity to meet and mix with other professionals who understand completely the issues childminders face on a daily basis. Support groups offer the chance to share views and ideas.

Many support groups are run from local premises such as church halls, scout huts, sports centres etc or sometimes each others' homes. It is worth enquiring whether your own area has a support group and go along to introduce yourself. Support groups can also offer a good opportunity to get yourself and your business known. If you have any vacancies, you can mention it to the other childminders in your group and if they get enquiries that they cannot fill they may be happy to pass your details on to prospective customers.

The National Childminding Association

The National Childminding Association (NCMA) is the *only* organisation in this country that has been specifically set up for the benefit of childminders.

The NCMA has a national network of development workers and staff whose job it is to promote the quality of childminding. The NCMA regularly liaises with the government on behalf of childminders to improve the conditions and status of this valuable service.

Network co-ordinators

There are many childminding networks throughout the country and each network has its own co-ordinator. Network co-ordinators are an invaluable source of information with regard to availability of training courses in your area and are often a point of contact for potential customers seeking a childminder. It is a good idea to give your details to your local co-ordinator and ensure she is aware of any vacancies you have.

Support childminders

The support childminding project is a new scheme set up to help newly-qualified childminders, or those working through their registration, for up to a year into their new careers. Many childminders, new to the profession, are confused and feel out on a limb once their registration has been granted. They may need someone to talk to who can offer help, advice or reassurance. The government has offered some local councils funding to develop support childminding schemes, where experienced childminders can use their expertise to offer the necessary support and advice to newly-qualified childminders.

Support childminders can offer help by telephone, e-mail or face-to-face meetings. Support childminders must be working as childminders themselves and they will have had special training in knowing how to support others in the profession. They will be able to help you with the day-to-day running of your own business, advise you on everything that is happening in your own area, and introduce you to support groups, drop-in centres, toy libraries etc.

Local authority

Local authorities have set up Early Years Development and Child Care Partnerships (EYDCP). Many of these partnerships employ staff who are responsible solely for childminders. They offer help and advice to childminders and are a useful source of support. They can provide details of training courses in your area and can put you in touch with social services, child protection officers etc.

Health visitors

Health visitors are knowledgeable in the growth and development of children. If you feel there is a particular problem with a child you care for, a health visitor can offer help and advice. They can put you and the parents in touch with other professionals who will be able to help, such as therapists and specialists. Remember that it is very important that you seek parental permission before contacting a child's health visitor.

Teachers

If you care for school-aged children part of your job will be liaising with a child's teachers. If you are taking and collecting the child every day then it is highly unlikely that their parents will be in a position to speak to the school themselves and it is therefore your duty to do this for them. The parents may have a particular concern that they may ask you to mention to their child's teacher and if this is the case you must handle the situation sensitively and convey the information accurately and confidentially.

The learning opportunities you provide for school-aged children should support the work they do in school and you should encourage and help children with any homework they bring to your setting. If a child is struggling with their homework, you must inform the parent and decide together what support is required.

Family

Last, but by no means least, a very important method of support for all childminders is the child's own family. It is important that you understand that *no one* knows a child better than their own parents. If you have any worries or concerns about a child in your care, the first people you should speak to are the child's own parents (except in cases of suspected abuse when it would not be in the child's own interests to inform a parent of your concerns). It is important that you discuss your concerns with the parents and work out, together, what needs to be done.

Your own family can also be a valuable source of support. Before starting out in your career as a childminder you should discuss all the problems which may be associated with your venture and your own family will, hopefully, agree then to support you. Childminding is a very demanding career and, coupled with the pressures of your own family life, it can be exhausting unless you get support from your own partner and children. It is important to remember though that confidentiality issues extend to your own family and it is not wise to discuss matters relating to the families of the children you care for with anyone, not even your own partner. Your own family can support you in other ways, such as helping around the house, tidying up, shopping or carrying out DIY projects as and when necessary.

◆ TIP ◆

No one knows children as well as their parents do. It is important to remember that although you may care for a child full time their parents are still the people who know them best. Never try to undermine a parent's decision, unless you really feel it is in the child's best interests to do so.

9

Providing Play and
Other Stimulating Activities

WHAT IS PLAY?

If asked, I am sure that most people would associate the word 'play' with images of entertainment and amusement. Of course there are many words which could describe play but in general it is having fun either alone or with others.

◆ TIP ◆

One of the most important ways in which children learn is through play and it is important that you are aware of and understand the many different forms of play.

Play is not something that only children are capable of, nor is it age related. Play is a way of unwinding and relaxing. Contrary to many people's beliefs, children do not know how to play 'naturally'. They are in fact taught how to play, either by the adults around them or the children they are with. It is therefore vital that you understand the importance of play and how to offer appropriate activities to stimulate the children in your care.

DIFFERENT TYPES OF PLAY

Apart from the obvious indoor and outdoor differences of play there are many other variations. Play for the children in your care will usually take one of two forms:

Structured play

This is when you have *planned* the play beforehand. You will have decided on the activity and thought about the learning outcomes you are hoping to achieve.

For example, it might take the form of introducing coloured building blocks. The child could be encouraged to develop colour recognition by building towers of perhaps all red bricks followed by all blue bricks.

Spontaneous play

This is when the children are allowed to play freely. They decide for themselves which activity they are going to do and choose the props, if any, they are intending to use.

Spontaneous play could, for example, take the form of role play. You provide the child with the dressing-up clothes and necessary props and they use their imagination to decide who they are going to dress up as – and the play develops spontaneously.

CATEGORIES OF PLAY

In addition to being structured or spontaneous, play falls into different categories.

Manipulative play

This includes activities such as:

♦ **Jigsaw puzzles.** A variety of puzzles should be provided with wooden pieces and board pieces in different shapes and sizes.

♦ **Painting** with a variety of instruments such as brushes, sponges, rollers, etc and with powder paint, ready-mixed paint and finger paint.

♦ **Crayoning** with a variety of instruments such as wax and pencil crayons, chalks and felt tip pens. Crayons and pencils should be of varying sizes.

- **Cooking**. Simple no-cook recipes can be enjoyed with even very young children. They can be encouraged to weigh, add and mix the ingredients.

- **Construction toys and building bricks**. A selection of construction toys of varying sizes should be provided and building bricks of an appropriate size, depending on the age of the child for example, Lego, Duplo or Sticklebricks.

Imaginative play

This includes activities such as:

- **Role play**. Dressing-up clothes and props should be provided for the children to explore.

- **Dolls and puppets**. Finger puppets, dolls, prams, doll's house and other small world toys could be provided.

- **Painting and drawing**. See previously. This activity is a valuable way for children to express themselves.

Creative play

This includes activities such as:

- **Painting and drawing**. See previously.

- **Play dough**. This could be shop bought or home made and it is a good idea to provide baking cutters or other plastics templates.

- **Model making**. Children should be supplied with a variety of boxes, cardboard and other junk material to allow them to create their own models.

- **Books/videos/music/rhymes**. Books are a vital part of learning for children and it is a good idea to have a selection of books for children of all ages. These can vary from cloth books and board books for the very young through to references books and picture dictionaries for school-aged children. Videos are a way of relaxing and enjoying quiet time, and they can also be educational. Songs and rhymes are a good way of introducing music to children and you could add to this by providing simple instruments such as tambourines, maracas, drums etc. Actions can be taught to go with many rhymes and songs.

◆ **Sand and water**. You may prefer to limit this activity to outdoors but it is vital to realise the importance of this particular activity. Children love to explore sand and water. Provide them with a variety of instruments such as measuring jugs, sieves, scoops etc.

◆ TIP ◆

Learn when to become involved in a child's play and when to allow them the freedom to explore and enjoy alone.

Outdoor play and physical exercise

This includes activities such as:

◆ **Obstacle courses**. These can be planned either for outdoors or in. Obstacles such as cones, hoops, bean bags, skittles, etc can be arranged for the children to negotiate.

◆ **Ride-on toys**.

◆ **Physical exercise** such as jumping, hopping, skipping, etc. Older children can be encouraged to play games of football, tennis, etc.

The above is only the tip of the iceberg when it comes to providing play and activities for children and you will discover many alternatives and additions as your childminding career progresses.

It is important to remember that, although you must provide a good selection of appropriate toys and plan activities to suit the children, *you* are the best toy the children can have! Children learn from the adults around them and you must give the appropriate amount of time and attention that each individual child needs.

10

Child Protection

TYPES AND SIGNS OF ABUSE

One of the most important aspects of a childminder's job is to ensure that the children in their care are safe at all times. It is your duty to ensure that your premises, both inside and out, are free from any potential dangers and that you practice safe methods. There may, however, be times when you suspect that a child is being exposed to danger and ill-treatment when they are away from your setting and if this is the case you must act on your suspicions.

In order to be able to effectively ascertain whether or not a child is being mistreated it is important that you have a basic knowledge of the types and signs of abuse and that you are aware of the procedures you must follow if you suspect that a child is being abused.

◆ TIP ◆

Never ignore the signs of abuse. You have a duty and responsibility to ensure that any child you care for is safe and protected. If you suspect a child is being abused you *must* do something about it. The child's welfare must be your priority at *all* times.

There is no set pattern for child abuse. It can happen to any child in any family structure. Abuse does not discriminate. It does not occur just in poor families or single parent families but in 'respectable' families and to children who appear to come from loving, affluent homes.

If you decide to extend your training qualifications and go on to complete the Certificate In Childminding Practice and NVQ 3 in Children's Care,

Learning and Development you will cover, in detail, aspects of child abuse. However if you do not go on to complete these qualifications, you must still be aware of the signs and symptoms associated with child abuse.

Neglect

This is when a child does not receive the appropriate care required for them to grow and develop. Neglect can come in a variety of ways, for example the child may be deprived of sufficient food, adequate clothing or medical care. A neglected child is not necessarily unloved. It may be that the child's parents have issues of their own and these problems may be preventing them from caring for their child adequately.

Signs of neglect

- underweight;
- tired and listless;
- inappropriately dressed for the weather conditions;
- dirty with poor skin conditions, matted unclean hair, and persistent nappy rash in a baby;
- frequent health problems;
- frequent accidents;
- the child telling you that they are often left alone, perhaps in charge of siblings;
- parents who are often unable to be reached and who persistently fail to keep appointments with health visitors, teachers etc.

Physical abuse

This is caused by an adult injuring a child through hitting, shaking, burning, using excessive force or poisoning.

Signs of physical abuse

- frequent, unexplained injuries such as bruises, cuts and grazes;
- bite marks;
- scalds or burns;
- frequent broken bones;
- lack of appetite;

- lack of interest in surroundings and activities, becoming withdrawn;
- showing aggression towards others;
- lacking self-esteem;
- delayed development.

Sexual abuse

This is when a child is used by an adult for their own sexual gratification. Sexual abuse can vary; it can include rape and involving children in pornography. Most cases of sexual abuse towards children are carried out by an adult who is known to the child.

Signs of sexual abuse

- non-accidental bruises and scratches, particularly around the buttocks and genital area;
- bloodstains and discharge in underwear;
- difficulty in going to the toilet, frequent 'accidents';
- difficulty walking or sitting down;
- frequent infections of the genitals;
- showing signs of distress;
- becoming clingy and withdrawn;
- inappropriate use of language and abnormal sexual behaviour;
- showing signs of comfort behaviour such as rocking or needing a comforter such as a dummy which are inappropriate for the age of the child;
- exposing themselves inappropriately;
- play which is of an inappropriate sexual nature;
- drawings or paintings of a sexual nature;
- unusual fascination with sexual behaviour;
- lack of appetite, unable to settle.

Emotional abuse

This is when a child is continually threatened verbally, either by being shouted at or put down. A child is also emotionally abused if their parent fails to show them adequate love and affection.

Signs of emotional abuse

- attention seeking, either by being deliberately uncooperative, telling lies or causing trouble within the setting;
- clinging to an adult;
- resorting to tantrums;
- having low self-esteem;
- constantly putting themselves down and commenting that they are worthless;
- having eating problems;
- resorting to self harm.

Recognising the signs

It is important to realise that there are other signs of abuse and you must be vigilant when carrying out your childminding duties. You must also bear in mind that some of the above mentioned signs, such as lack of appetite and restlessness, can also be experienced if a child is unwell. Obviously you must take illness into account when considering the facts. It is also important to remember that some birthmarks can look like bruises and some rashes may give the appearance that a child has been slapped.

Often people are afraid to get involved with cases of child abuse, either because they are worried about the effect it may have on their own lives or because they are not completely certain of the facts. However, it is vital that if you have any concerns, you report your suspicions to the appropriate authorities. It is important to realise that whilst cases of child abuse are rare, they do happen and you have to be confident when handling these situations.

◆ TIP ◆

Remember most children will suffer, at some time in their lives, from cuts and bruises due to falls. These injuries are *usually* on the forehead, chin, knee or shin.

You should be concerned if a child in your care has persistent injuries to the following areas of their body:

- ◆ back;
- ◆ buttocks;
- ◆ back of the legs;
- ◆ eyes;
- ◆ ears;
- ◆ cheeks;
- ◆ mouth;
- ◆ neck;
- ◆ rectal and genital areas;
- ◆ stomach;
- ◆ chest;
- ◆ upper and inner arms.

Injuries to the above parts of the body are not *usually* associated with accidents. As with all checklists, the above is not perfect and it only provides an indication of what may constitute signs of physical abuse. Injuries to the above mentioned parts of the body are only signs that abuse may have taken place. The most important thing you, as a childminder, can do, is to be aware of the signs and record anything you observe which may be of concern. By noting down your observations you will easily notice if a pattern emerges or if a child in your care repeatedly suffers from injuries that cannot easily be explained.

If you become suspicious that a child in your care is being abused, you must follow your own Area Child Protection Committee procedure. You will be made aware of this procedure when you apply to be registered and you complete the compulsory course, Introduction to Childminding Practice.

If a child divulges information to you about an incident of child abuse, listen to them carefully and offer lots of reassurance. Tell them they have done the right thing by confiding in you and let them know that you are going to help them. *Never* promise to keep the information a secret. You will *not* be able to keep this promise and you will be letting down an already very vulnerable child who has trusted you and confided in you.

ALLEGATIONS AGAINST CHILDMINDERS

As a childminder you need to be aware of the possibility that someone may accuse you or a member of your family of abusing a child in your care. This is a rare occurrence but it is important that you are aware of the possible implications and what you need to do to protect yourself and your family against any such allegations.

An allegation of abuse against a childminder or a member of the childminder's family may come about because parents are trying to cover up their own abuse of their children. In cases like this it is important that you do *not* discuss your suspicions with the parents – always contact another professional first.

The teenage sons of childminders are particularly vulnerable to accusations of child abuse and it is important that, because you work alone, you are aware of just how vulnerable you are to allegations. There are ways that you can protect yourself and your family from allegations of child abuse:

Maintain records
Maintain accurate, up-to-date records of all accidents and incidents to children in your care, and ensure that the parents sign your written record. Maintain accurate, up-to-date records of all injuries to a child *arriving* at your home. If you notice an injury ask the parents to explain what happened and record this in your accident book, and get the parent to sign it to show that they accept what you have noticed.

Report your concerns
Ensure that any concerns you may have about the welfare of a child in your care are reported to the appropriate authorities. Keep a written record of the nature of the suspected abuse and your conversations with the authority in question. Record the date and time of the conversation, who you spoke to and the action agreed.

Your children
Make sure that you never allow your own children to be left alone with any of the childminded children in your care.

Confidentiality
Maintain confidentiality at all times.

Tell the parents
Make sure that you tell parents of any accident to a child in your care, however insignificant it may seem. Also, ensure that you tell parents if you notice any sudden changes in their child's behaviour or if they appear to be using inappropriate language or play.

Your behaviour
Always make sure that *you* use appropriate language when in the presence of the children and *never* resort to rough treatment when managing a child's unwanted behaviour.

Physical affection
Allow children to ask you for cuddles rather than you asking them.

Encourage independence
Encourage children to become independent as soon as possible, particularly when they are carrying out personal tasks such as going to the toilet, getting changed etc.

Encourage honesty
Encourage children to be honest and teach them not to keep secrets. However, *never* push them to divulge information they are not happy to tell you and do not put words into their mouth. If a child does tell you about an incident, allow them to tell you in their own words; do not rush them. Offer them lots of reassurance and tell them they have done the right thing by telling you.

Keep informed

Make sure that you keep your training up to date and attend child protection courses to ensure that you are well-informed of the procedures you may need to take if you suspect a child is being abused.

Safety for children

Teach children how to be safe and how to protect themselves. Teach them about 'stranger danger' and the importance of telling an adult where they are going, who they are going with and when they will be back.

Coping with allegations

Having allegations made against you or a member of your family can be a very distressing experience, and it is important that you remain calm and professional at all times. Make sure that you keep records of all the conversations you have relating to the allegation and keep copies of all the letters or e-mails you send. If you are a member of the National Childminding Association you should inform them immediately of any accusation made against you. They will be able to offer legal help and advice. If you are not a member of the NCMA, then you can seek independent advice from the Citizens Advice Bureau.

Dealing with any case of child abuse, whether the allegations are made against you, your family or someone else entirely, will have a strain on you and the way you conduct your business. You will experience a variety of feelings – anger against the abuser, hurt and upset if the allegations are made against you, shock at what has happened to the child and guilt at not having noticed that something was wrong. All these feelings are perfectly natural and you need to know how to handle them and where you can turn for support to help *you* through this difficult situation. It is important to remember that any cases of suspected child abuse are confidential; however you can seek support from:

+ child protection officers;
+ social workers;
+ health visitors and GPs;
+ the NSPCC;
+ Kidscape.

11

Causes for Complaint

The relationship between childminder, parents and child is often a close one as you are working in partnership together to provide the best possible childcare. It is crucial that you remember that parents are the most important people in their child's life, and you must understand and respect their wishes. You may become very good friends with the parents of the children you care for and remain in contact with them long after their children have grown up and left your childcare setting. This is one of the most rewarding aspects of childminding. However, it is still important to remember that you are running a business and whilst you can be good friends with your customers your relationship with them must also be on a business and financial level.

WHEN THINGS GO WRONG

No matter how hard you work, how many hours you devote to other people's children and how many training courses you undertake there is no foolproof way of ensuring that you will never receive a complaint. This is quite simply because, as the saying goes, 'You can not please all of the people all of the time.' You will, over time, learn how to juggle your work with running your home and looking after your own family. I will not pretend that it is easy when there are many demands on your time. Sometimes you will feel that there are not enough hours in the day. There will be times when your best laid plans fall by the wayside and you feel as if you are meeting yourself coming backwards but this can, and does, happen in all workplaces. The important thing to remember is that you are a professional person doing a professional job and you must act the part at all times. Even when you feel that whatever you say or do is not good enough, and there will be times when this is the case, you must bite your tongue, remain polite and refrain from passing judgement.

DEALING WITH CONFLICT

It is important to remember that working parents may feel an element of guilt at having to leave their children and, when they are stressed and tired after a long day, it is sometimes all too easy to say something hurtful or insensitive. Try not to dwell on this or read too much into it.

However, that is not to say that you must sit back and be insulted. Being a professional does not mean being a doormat. It is possible for you to get your message across without an argument. Just as a parent has the right to say something if they are not happy with a particular element of the childcare service you are providing, you too have the right to let them know if you feel that they are continually taking advantage of your good nature.

Late collections

If, for example, a parent turns up late one evening to collect their child and tells you that there was an accident on the motorway, there is every chance that this is the case and the delay in getting to you was therefore unavoidable. However, if the same parent continually turns up late, with no valid reasons, and you have to rearrange your own family commitments accordingly, it is not advisable to keep quiet. By not confronting the parent you will become resentful, your family life will suffer, and you will not be able to carry out your childminding duties properly.

◆ **TIP** ◆

Do not allow tension and resentment to build up. Always tackle a problem calmly and honestly.

Tell the parent why you need them to collect their child on time; perhaps your own daughter has to be at her piano lesson, or you have a training course to attend, and the parent collecting their child late regularly is having an adverse effect on your own life. Remember that as a self-employed person, you choose the days and times that *you* want to work. You will have set your daily working hours according to your own family commitments and there may be valid reasons why you must stick to these times as much as possible. Of course you do need to be flexible.

◆ TIP ◆

Many parents chose a childminder over a nursery for the degree of flexibility they offer, but you must still not allow yourself to be taken advantage of. Most privately owned day nurseries are not flexible when it comes to closing times and they charge a premium rate for late collections.

Negotiating with parents

The best way to deal with a problem of this nature is to address it calmly. Do not be rude to the parent as they rush through the door or comment that your daughter will miss her music lesson yet again, due to their lack of time keeping. Instead choose a time when neither of you are in a hurry and, calmly and politely, point out that your working day finishes at a set time, which was agreed when you both signed your contract. Explain that you are not trying to be difficult but that you have family commitments, and that these are suffering because of the regular late evenings you are expected to work. (It may be that you do not have plans for the evenings but if this is the case you should still not be expected to work overtime regularly without recognition.)

Reaching an agreement

If you are willing to extend your working hours then tell the parent this and suggest that you agree a revised fee for the additional time worked, amend the contract and sign it together. However, if a late finishing time is completely inconvenient and you do not want to work these hours, even with extra payment, then inform the parent of your decision. Their reasons for being late may be genuinely unavoidable and by discussing the problem with them you may be able to come to a compromise; perhaps by agreeing to work late two evenings per week, with advance warning, or for the parent to arrange for their child to be collected by someone other than themselves.

◆ TIP ◆

> Look at your childminding business as a job. In many aspects a very enjoyable and extremely rewarding job, but it must not take precedence over your own family and life.

Everyone needs time away from work and how and where you spend your leisure time is your own business. However, I have found that by talking to the parents you can quickly and easily work out a solution to most everyday problems. Tackling a problem or unacceptable situation calmly and reasonably usually has promising results and I have found that very few parents try to be awkward, and the vast majority are remarkably accommodating.

Being open and approachable

You must make sure that all the parents of the children in your care can approach you at any time, if they want to discuss the care their child is receiving or any problems or difficulties they or their children are having. If it is not appropriate for them to discuss things with you immediately because, for example, other parents are collecting children at the same time and confidentiality is difficult, then arrange for them to telephone you later in the evening at a mutually convenient time. Or if they live nearby, ask them to call back later in the evening when you can sit down together and discuss any issues.

◆ TIP ◆

> A complaint should not always be seen in a negative light. There is often a valuable lesson to be learnt.

It could be that one of you has an issue with the childcare arrangements and it is crucial that, whatever the problem, it is dealt with promptly and professionally. If a problem is left to fester and grow out of proportion people will begin to feel resentful and the whole important relationship between childminder, parent and child can irreparably break down.

Always be honest and open with parents and never promise something you cannot or will not do. If you do not want to work weekends, for example, never hint that this is a possibility simply in order to fill a vacancy; it will, at a later date, mean that you resent losing your weekends or that you let down the parents should weekend cover be required. This is a bad start to a working relationship and should be avoided at all costs.

DIFFICULT PEOPLE AND SITUATIONS

There are probably times in your life when you have looked back and thought you could have avoided a certain situation if only you had handled things differently. I am sure every one of us can think of at least one occasion that we would not wish to repeat and would, in hindsight, have avoided at all costs if we had been better prepared. Handling difficult people and situations is an everyday fact of life. We are all different; we all want and need different things and we all have a different outlook on life. It is these differences which make us all unique. It is often all too easy to see things through our own eyes and we tend to base our opinions of other people on the things we see, rather than on the whole picture.

Making judgements
Often we do not get to know someone completely; we are only aware of the things they choose to share with us. It is very easy to make assumptions about a person which can be completely unfounded and totally unfair. For example, you may be met each morning with a mother who is, in your opinion, curt or abrupt. She may drop her child off with you and rush out without passing the time of day. You could be forgiven for thinking that she was career minded and focused on her work that she was rude and uncaring about the welfare of her child. This assumption could be right but it could also just as easily be very wrong. The parent

- may feel **guilty** at leaving her child and therefore find it easier to rush away so as not to prolong the departure for both herself and her child;
- she may be **shy and unsure** of what is expected of her;
- she may be **worried about something** that she has not confided in you.

There are many reasons for a person to act in a certain way and we should not be quick to stand in judgement.

Some people are, of course, naturally rude or arrogant and hopefully if you encounter someone like this you will be able to decide, prior to the placement commencement and ideally at the first meeting, whether or not you feel you are able to provide a service for a family of this nature. First impressions are very important and it is often possible to decide whether or not you like a person's 'nature' during the initial meeting you have with them.

◆ TIP ◆

Constructive criticism can be very helpful. Often someone can come up with an idea that you had simply not thought of but which could be beneficial to the everyday running of your business. Always listen to other people's advice before deciding whether to heed it.

Later problems

Some people, however, seem perfectly amicable to begin with, and do not start to show their true colours until later on, after the contract has been signed and the placement has begun. The signing of the contract, although a legally binding document, still does not stop parents treating you unreasonably. But in my experience as a childminder I think I can honestly say that, if you are providing a good service and have an easy, open relationship with the children and their parents, you should not have too much difficulty remaining on good terms with them. It is important to remember to be fair and as flexible as possible whilst seeing things from all sides. If you sense a problem or you feel things need clarifying then approach the parent in a polite, professional manner. Never raise your voice or lose your temper, even if they do.

◆ TIP ◆

Often, complaints come about when one person or another doesn't completely understand what is expected of them. It is very important to express yourself clearly and listen to others carefully to eliminate any misunderstandings.

There may however, still be times when you feel that you can no longer continue to provide childcare for a particular family. The decision to terminate the contract could come from either party. If you feel the need to terminate the contract, I would advise you to discuss the problem with the parent and try to resolve the issue first of all. Failing this, explain why you feel the need to terminate the contract and agree a date for termination. This should have been stated on the contract but you may agree to a shorter or longer period of notice, depending on the circumstances of the family and nature of the grievance.

CONTRACT DISPUTES

Protecting children

Children are very adept at knowing when things are not right between adults. They can sense an atmosphere and may become stressed if they feel that the important adults in their lives are not getting on well. It is important to avoid any kind of bad feeling for this reason. Although a child may sense a grievance they may not be old enough to understand the reason behind it. Ignoring a conflict or refusing to discuss it can be very harmful to your business. Other parents and children may sense a problem and wonder why there is tension between you and another parent. Confidentiality procedures will prevent you from discussing, with someone else, any problems which do not concern them.

Clarifying the contract

One of the most important things you must do, prior to a placement commencing, is to sit down with the parents of the child and go through the contract with them. The contract you provide, and its contents, must be clearly explained to the parents and any questions they may have must be answered honestly, prior to signing. We have looked at contracts in more detail in Chapter 6. It should clearly outline the service you are prepared to provide and cover aspects such as:

◆ days and hours you are available;
◆ fees you charge;
◆ holiday arrangements;

◆ illness arrangements;

◆ arrangements for playgroup, nursery and school collections.

Basically, any important aspects of the service you provide, and any additional requests made by the parents, should be recorded on the contract. It is better to put too much information into a contract than too little, and the accuracy and detail you provide at this stage should alleviate any misunderstandings in the future. *All* parties concerned must be aware of, and fully understand, what is expected of them prior to signing the contract. Providing parents with copies of your policies (discussed in Chapter 8), will help to back up your requirements and avoid future disputes.

The necessity for a contract

There are a number of reasons why you need to have a contract between yourself and the parents of the children you are providing care for.

◆ A written contract sets out exactly what is expected of both yourself and the parents of the children you are caring for.

◆ A contract is a legally binding document. If you have problems in the future regarding aspects such as non payment of fees, it is very important to have a contract if you are intending to recover unpaid costs.

◆ Having a contract puts your business on a professional level. A contract can be tailormade to meet the needs of each individual family and shows you are committed to providing a good professional service.

The contract, once signed, is a legally binding document and for this reason everyone concerned must be aware of what they are putting their signature to. The document should state the childcare arrangements which you have agreed to provide for a negotiated fee, under agreed terms and conditions. It is *not* a contract of employment.

Breakdown in communication

Contract disputes usually come about when there has been a breakdown in communication between the parent and the childminder. As I have mentioned before it is important that you discuss, wherever possible, any problems as and when they arise. Ignoring a problem will not make it go away but it could well make it escalate out of all proportion making it impossible for a solution to be found. Although prompt action should be taken to deal with any problems which may, from time to time, arise, you must make sure that you do not act impulsively.

Reaching a compromise
Take time to think the situation through, and if possible, try to find several compromises which you would be happy with and which you could put to the parent for consideration. You will probably find that if you are open to suggestions and willing to compromise then a solution can be found rather than if you are completely adamant and unwilling to show flexibility.

It may take several discussions before a problem is resolved and you may decide to try a particular course of action, monitor the response and review it at a later date. However, in some cases (thankfully in my experience this is rare) you may have to terminate the contract. There may be certain circumstances when one, or both, parties are unable to find a compromise and it would not be beneficial from the child's, the parents', or your business' point of view to continue with the contract.

AREAS OF CONFLICT

It is worth taking the time to think about the areas which you feel may bring conflict to your childminding setting. By thinking of the different issues in advance you will be better prepared to handle any situations as and when they arise.

Some of the most common areas involving conflict when working as a childminder are:

◆ disputes over pay and working hours;
◆ concerns over day-to-day duties and responsibilities;
◆ disputes over the daily routines of the children;
◆ disagreements over differing parenting practices and family lifestyles;

- disputes concerning prejudice or discrimination;
- changes in family circumstances e.g. divorce.

Most of the above areas can be dealt with by using a detailed, accurate contract and by ensuring that everyone completely understands what is expected of them. Childminding is largely about negotiation and compromise. You, and the parents of the children in your care, must realise that some degree of compromise has to be made by *everyone*. Parents must be aware that if you care for several children it is not always easy to accommodate their every whim and sometimes solutions have to be found.

When dealing with any areas of conflict or disagreement, *always*:

- Remain calm and professional – never raise your voice, even if the parents do. You are much more likely to be heard if you lower your voice!

- Be tactful. Refrain from being rude or making unnecessary comments which appear to criticise the parents.

- Make sure that you have the facts at hand. Try not to throw lots of niggling grievances at the parent when addressing an important concern. Focus on the exact issue which needs to be dealt with.

- Avoid acting hastily – give yourself, and the parents, time to calm down and collect your thoughts before tackling an issue.

- Try to offer as many solutions to the problem as possible and, if possible, be prepared to compromise.

◆ TIP ◆

If you are caring for a child whose parents have recently divorced *never* take sides. Be prepared to help *everyone* concerned. Offer additional childcare if necessary but refrain, at all costs, from getting involved in the marriage breakdown. It is your job to provide continuity of care for the child, not marriage guidance counselling for the parents! *Never* break confidentiality procedures by discussing a family's circumstances with anyone else.

Some things to remember when dealing with conflict during your working day:

◆ Be professional and ensure that you provide a positive role model to both the children and their parents.

◆ Stay calm, listen and offer sympathy, support and reassurance when necessary.

◆ Ensure you are non-judgemental and avoid stereotyping.

◆ Remain positive and helpful. Be prepared to compromise whenever possible.

◆ Never become aggressive or abusive.

◆ TIP ◆

Childminders should work in partnership with parents at all times to ensure that the children's best interests are put first.

12

Your Inspection

Registration and inspections used to be carried out by the local authority but in 2001 this was transferred to the Ofsted directorate. It is the job of Ofsted inspectors to look at, and monitor, the ways in which childcare providers demonstrate how they meet the English National Standards (these standards are covered in depth in Chapter 2). Childminders practising in Northern Ireland, Scotland and Wales will need to follow the guidelines for the standards in their own areas. (See useful contacts at the end of the book.)

Ofsted has the power to investigate your setting as a childminder to ensure that you are meeting the standards and can request that changes are made if necessary. Ofsted also has the power to terminate your registration if your setting does not conform to the national standards.

THE GRADING SYSTEM

In April 2005 Ofsted announced that they would change some of the ways in which they inspect childcare settings in England.

One of the areas of change is the grading system. In the past, childminders' inspection reports have stated that the childcare service provided is either 'good', 'satisfactory' or 'unsatisfactory'. The grading proved unpopular and confusing and has now been replaced with a new, four-tier scale of:

Grade 1 Outstanding: given to exceptional settings that have excellent outcomes for children.

Grade 2 Good: given to strong settings that are effective in promoting outcomes for children.

Grade 3 Satisfactory: given to settings that have acceptable outcomes for children but have scope for improvement.

Grade 4 Inadequate: given to weak settings that have unacceptable outcomes for children.

In addition to the changes in the grading scale, Ofsted now gives shorter notice periods prior to inspections and has introduced a simple self-assessment element to the inspection.

Inspection frameworks for childcare will be more in line with those of schools and colleges and reports will focus on what it is like to be a child in that particular day-care setting. In order for the inspector to judge the overall quality of the care you provide, Ofsted inspectors will base their judgement on how well you meet a series of outcomes for children which are set out in the green paper, 'Every Child Matters', and are now in the Children Act 2004.

The points considered will be how you:

1. help children to be healthy;
2. protect them from harm or neglect and help them stay safe;
3. help them enjoy and achieve;
4. help them make a positive contribution to your provision and the wider community.

Inspectors will also base their assessments on how well you organise your childcare to help promote children's well-being and look at whether you meet the National Standards (see Chapter 2).

HOW TO MEET THE STANDARDS SUCCESSFULLY

Few people, no matter how good the service they provide, or how many years they have been providing childcare, relish the idea of an inspection. The idea of having your work assessed, your moves monitored and your words scrutinised can fill even the most confident childminder with dread. However, inspections are a vital part of your work and it is essential that you plan properly for your Ofsted visit.

Your home and work will already be scrutinised on a daily basis, probably without you even realising it, when parents drop off and collect their children from you. No matter how tired and harassed the parent may be don't be fooled into thinking they will not notice if *you* are short tempered or if your house is dirty or the children are unhappy. They will, and most importantly, they should! If your business lives up to the watchful eye of your parents then you should rest assured that Ofsted will have an equally high opinion of your provision. However, it is vital that you are aware of the National Standards and how to implement them, not just during your inspection visit but throughout all your working hours. These standards are available from Ofsted and they give information about the standards themselves, points for consideration, what the inspector looks for during an inspection and the things they base their judgements on. (We looked at them in detail in Chapter 2.)

The Ofsted inspector will look at each of the National Standards and expect to see you meeting them successfully. Below are some of the things the inspector will be looking for during their visit.

Standard One – Suitable Person

- Your training and first aid qualifications.
- The procedures you follow when employing an assistant or if you work with a fellow childminder.
- Your arrangements for protecting children against people on your premises who have not been vetted.
- Any changes to your working circumstances since your last inspection.

Standard Two – Organisation

- The way you store your records.
- Accurate record of attendance.
- The adult:child ratios being maintained.
- The way children are cared for, ensuring they have sufficient adult interaction.
- Adult support enabling them to feel secure, happy and confident.
- The way you utilise your space and resources

Standard Three – Care, Learning and Play

- How you decide which activities to provide.
- How you organise your activities.
- How you promote children's development using the toys and equipment you provide.

Standard Four – Physical Environment

- Which rooms are accessible to children.
- How you organise your space.
- Your telephone access.
- Your kitchen.
- Your nappy changing facilities and toilet.
- Your outdoor area (if you have one) and the arrangements you make for outdoor exercise.
- Your planning permission (if applicable).

Standard Five – Equipment

- How you ensure that your toys and equipment are safe.
- How you ensure that your toys and equipment are suitable for the age and development of the children in your care.
- That your toys and resources are stimulating and challenging.
- That you have sufficient toys and equipment to ensure all the children in your care are comfortable and that they can eat and play together.

Standard Six – Safety

- Your plans for fire safety and emergency evacuation.
- Your smoke alarms and fire blanket.
- Your arrangements for outings.
- Public liability insurance.
- Records for any vehicles and drivers.
- Any recommendations made by the fire safety officer.
- How safe and secure your home and outdoor area are.

Standard Seven – Health

- Your accident and medication records.
- Medication and emergency treatment records.

- Your first aid box.
- The arrangements you make for sick children.

Standard Eight – Food and Drink

- The records you have concerning children's dietary needs.
- How you enquire about, and subsequently meet, the dietary needs of the children in your care.
- Your arrangements for providing food and drink.

Standard Nine – Equal Opportunities

- The records you keep for the children in your care.
- The way in which you enquire about children's needs.
- Your understanding of equality of opportunity.

Standard Ten – Special Needs

- The records you keep for the children in your care.
- Your arrangements for caring for children with special needs.
- The way in which you share information about your provision with parents of children with special needs.

Standard Eleven – Behaviour

- Records of any significant incidents.
- Your method of informing parents of how you manage behaviour.
- Your written arrangements with parents regarding behaviour.

Standard Twelve – Working in Partnership with Parents and Carers

- The information you share with parents about your routines, policies and procedures.
- Your contracts and records of payment.
- Records of any complaints.
- Children's and parents' records.

Standard Thirteen – Child Protection

- Children's records.
- That you are aware of the Area Child Protection Procedures.
- That you are completely aware of what child abuse and neglect are.

◆ The procedure you would follow if any allegations of abuse were made against you, anyone you may employ or any member of your family.

Standard Fourteen – Documentation
◆ The documents that you keep.
◆ Where you keep your documents and how long you retain them.
◆ Whether you notify Ofsted of any changes in your circumstances.

HOW OFTEN WILL MY SETTING BE INSPECTED?

Newly-registered childminders will usually have their first Ofsted inspection within a short period of time after their registration. After the initial inspection Ofsted will usually carry out further inspections at least once every three years. However in certain circumstances, as listed below, inspections will be more frequent.

◆ If the last inspection concluded that the quality of childcare you provide had significant weaknesses.

◆ If there have been significant changes to the setting since the last inspection, such as a change of premises.

◆ If a complaint has been made against you that suggests you are not meeting the National Standards.

WILL I KNOW MY INSPECTION DATE IN ADVANCE?

Ofsted wants to see your setting running as normally as possible on any given day without you having to make any special arrangements. However, they also realise that many childminders spend a large amount of their time out of the home on school runs, attending support groups, toddler sessions etc. So to avoid calling when you are not at home, the inspector will usually telephone a few days in advance to check whether there are any days in the coming week when it would not be suitable to visit.

WHAT THE INSPECTION INVOLVES

First of all, it is natural to feel a little nervous about your inspection particularly if you are a newly-qualified childminder and have had little or no experience in dealing with childcare inspections. Even those of us who have been childminding for many years still feel a little apprehensive about the inspection; after all someone is coming into your home to inspect and grade a service you are providing. It is important to remember that the inspector is not your enemy, they are simply doing their job and ensuring that the childcare you provide meets the necessary criteria set out by the Office for Standards in Education.

When an inspector arrives at your home it is important to carry on your normal routine without making any changes. Disruption should be kept to a minimum although, of course, you will need to be available to talk with the inspector when required. At the beginning you will be informed of how the inspection will be carried out. Usually, the inspector will:

- observe what the children and adults in the setting are doing;
- talk to the children and, if possible, the parents to find out their views on the childcare provided;
- check your premises and equipment to ensure that they are safe and suitable and how well they are used to promote the outcomes for children;
- check your written records, procedures and any other necessary documentation.

Throughout the inspection the inspector will make notes of their findings. When the inspection is complete, usually after about two hours, they will let you know the outcome of their findings. You will normally see a display of the inspector's judgements on a laptop computer and these will be included in your final report. At this point you may correct factual information or ask for further clarification of any of the points the inspector raises.

What happens after the inspection

After your inspection you will be sent an inspection report. If there are any factual errors in the report at this stage you must inform Ofsted immediately as the report will be published on the Internet shortly after. The report, when published on the Internet, will not include your name or your full address.

WHAT HAPPENS IF THE QUALITY OF CARE IS CONSIDERED INADEQUATE

If your childcare provision is judged as 'satisfactory' or 'good' the report will include recommendations to help you to improve your provision further. The inspector will check whether these recommendations have been implemented at your next inspection (within three years from the date of the last one). However, if the inspector considers that the quality of care you are providing is inadequate then it will be because you are failing to meet one or more of the National Standards. If this judgement is made, Ofsted will do one of two things.

1. **Send you a letter to tell you what action you must take to improve the care you provide.** This letter is called a *notice of action to improve*. You will be required to let Ofsted know when you have taken the necessary action and an announced or unannounced visit may be carried out to check that the necessary improvements have been made. If you ignore the notice of action or the improvements you make have little impact on the outcome of your childcare provision, then Ofsted may take further enforcement measures. You will receive a further inspection within 6 to 12 months of the initial visit.

2. **Take enforcement action such as issuing you with a compliance notice** if your childcare provision is classed as poor and is considered in need of immediate improvement. An inspector will follow this notice up to ensure that the improvements have been made. In rare cases Ofsted may consider suspending or cancelling your registration. If Ofsted considers it necessary to take serious action against your setting, but still allows your registration to continue, then they will inspect your premises again either at the date given on any enforcement action or within 3 to 6 months, whichever is the sooner.

BEING READY FOR THE INSPECTION

Preparation is a key factor when anticipating your forthcoming inspection. No one can accurately guess exactly what will happen during an inspection – it will depend on the day the inspection takes place and which children you are caring for at the time. Even how the children are feeling on that particular day can have an impact on the way your inspection may go. If one of the children in your care is feeling a bit off colour or tired or simply refusing to cooperate it may add to the stress you are already feeling.

The important thing to remember is that the inspector understands that children rarely do exactly what they are expected to and it is how you *handle* any awkward or difficult situations that will be looked at. Try to relax and act as normally as possible. Go about your daily routines as you usually would and avoid making changes that would confuse or disrupt the children's usual patterns. After all, if you are complying with the requirements set out by Ofsted and are working within the National Standards all the time, which is what you should be doing, then you really have little to worry about.

There are a number of other points which you should consider to ensure that you are ready for your inspection. Make sure that:

- you and any assistants or other childminders you work with are familiar with all the relevant documents, such as the National Standards;

- you have put right any weaknesses identified in your last inspection report, if applicable;

- you have completed the self-evaluation form;

- you have all the records which the inspector will want to see (these are listed on the self-evaluation form);

- you keep any information about how parents view your service and any improvements you have made as a result. It is a good idea to produce a simple questionnaire to give to parents, prior to your inspection or periodically, say once a year, to establish how the parents of the children you care for view your setting and the childcare provision you provide.

Often constructive criticism can be very helpful and we all respond well to praise! There is an example of a questionnaire, which you could adapt to suit your own setting, below;

◆ you have available any records you keep of complaints about the childcare you provide;

◆ you have notified Ofsted of any significant changes you have made to your provision, for example any changes to the premises or people employed to look after the children.

QUESTIONNAIRE FOR PARENTS

In order that I can continue to provide a good quality childcare service that benefits all the children and their parents I would be much obliged if you would kindly take the time to complete this short questionnaire and return it to me as soon as possible.

1. Are you happy with the overall childcare I provide for your child/children?
2. If there are any improvements you feel I could make that would be of benefit to you, what would these be?
3. Are the hours I am available to work acceptable to you?
4. Are you happy with the meals I provide? Do you have any suggestions for improvements?
5. Are you happy with the activities I provide for your child/children? Do you think these could be improved in any way?
6. Do you consider that your child is happy in my setting and are there any ways I could make their time with me more enjoyable?
7. If your child/children are of school age do you consider that they get sufficient help from me with their homework/studies? Can you suggest any improvement?
8. Are you happy with the information I provide with regard to your child's daily routines? Is there any further information you would like?
9. Are there any further comments you would like to make which may help me to improve my daycare and before/after school service in order that all the children in my care remain happy and secure?

The above questionnaire can be adapted to suit your own childcare setting and it may be a good idea to distribute these periodically, especially if you have got new children starting. A good time to give a questionnaire out is just prior to renewing a contract so that any changes implemented can be reflected in the contract.

SELF-EVALUATION

Ofsted issues all childminders with a self-evaluation form prior to their planned inspection. The form sets out a series of questions and asks the childminder to grade themselves on the same scale as the inspector uses, i.e. grade 1: outstanding, grade 2: good, grade 3: satisfactory and grade 4: inadequate. You are asked the following questions:

1. How effective are you in helping children to be healthy?

2. How effective are you in protecting children from harm and neglect and keeping them safe?

3. How effective are you in helping children to enjoy what they do and to achieve as well as they can?

4. How effective are you in helping children make a positive contribution to your provision and to the wider community?

5. How effective is your organisation of childcare?

The self-evaluation form also lists the necessary documents you must have available to show the inspector during your inspection. These documents include the name, home address and date of birth of each child who is being cared for on the premises, contact details of parents/carers, records of accidents, records of medicine administered, attendance records etc.

13

Training

COMPULSORY TRAINING

Childminders in England are required to complete the mandatory course. At the time of writing this book, the course was entitled Introducing Childminding Practice (ICP). However, early in 2006 this course was altered to include *all* home based child carers such as nannies as well as childminders. The units which make up the Certificate in Childminding Practice are still recognised and it may be that you are already part way through one of the units so we will look at these in a little more detail in this chapter.

Introducing Childminding Practice was a mandatory course which childminders were required to undertake. ICP could be taken either as standard in a classroom or through a distance learning college. In January 2006 this course was amended to take into account all child carers working in a home based setting not just childminders. The new level three qualification is called the Diploma in Home-based Child Care.

First aid

In addition to the ICP all childminders in both England and Wales must take a pediatric first aid course. First aid courses for childminders have changed significantly over the years and it is now compulsory for childminders to be trained, in depth, in all areas of childcare first aid. Your local authority will be able to give you details of the requirements in your area together with dates and venues for suitable courses.

It is essential that you do not underestimate the importance of a first aid course, and to ensure that you keep your training up to date. This is also a compulsory requirement of Ofsted. First aid qualifications usually expire after three years. A first aid course will ensure you are fully prepared for any accident or emergency which you may encounter and it will give you the necessary training and confidence to deal with a situation professionally and proficiently. The National Childminding Association stipulates that a suitable first aid course for childminders should be at least 12 hours long in order to successfully cover all aspects of accidents and emergencies.

◆ **TIP** ◆

Ofsted requires *all* childminders to complete a comprehensive pediatric first aid course.

CERTIFICATE IN CHILDMINDING PRACTICE

The Certificate in Childminding Practice, or CCP as it was generally known, was made up of three separate units. The units could be completed individually but you would not achieve the CCP award unless you completed all three units. The units were:

- **Unit One**: Introducing Childminding Practice (ICP). This is the introductory course which we have just looked at.

- **Unit Two** Developing Childminding Practice (DCP).

- **Unit Three** Extending Childminding Practice (ECP).

The units followed on from one another and become more involved as they progressed. The complete certificate (CCP) was a level 3 qualification and was designed specifically for childminders. The award was developed by CACHE (Council for Awards in Children's Care and Education) and the National Childminding Association, and it is nationally recognised.

Unit Two: Developing Childminding Practice (DCP)

This course studied some of the topics covered in the ICP unit in more depth. DCP laid the foundations for the whole range of skills required by professional childminders.

Topics covered, in addition to those studied for in the ICP, were caring for babies and toddlers, children's development and working in partnership with parents.

This course was specifically designed for people already working with children so you had to be registered and caring for children in a home-based setting before enrolling on this course.

Unit Three: Extending Childminding Practice (ECP)

If you had successfully completed ICP and DCP this final course enabled you to gain CACHE's Level 3 Certificate in Childminding Practice.

ECP is aimed at experienced childminders and, like DCP, to study for this course you had to be registered and caring for children in a home-based setting. The course covered topics such as child development, working with professionals, supporting parents, and working with children affected by disability, behavioural or emotional difficulties, HIV, Aids or abuse.

The full CCP course was widely available throughout England and Wales at centres approved by CACHE. In addition to colleges and adult education centres, the National Childminding Association also offered the course in areas where funding for childminders' training was available.

It is also possible to complete the CCP as a distance learning course and was invaluable to childminders who work very long hours or shift patterns and found it difficult to attend classes. The National Extension College offers the complete CCP course and can be contacted by visiting www.nec.ac.uk/courses or telephoning 0800 3892839 for a prospectus.

As I mentioned earlier in this chapter the Certificate in Childminding Practice is in the process of being changed. At the time of writing, plans were being made for two new qualifications to come into effect from January 2006, namely the Level 2 Award/Certificate in Approved Child Carers and the Level 3 Diploma in Home-based Child Care. These courses differ from the Certificate in Childminding Practice as they take into account *all* individuals working with children in a home based setting such as nannies, as well as childminders.

The two new qualifications offered by CACHE are as follows:

Level 3 Diploma in Home-based Child Care – this course is made up of five units which are as follows:

Unit 1 Introduction to childcare practice (home-based)

Unit 2 Childcare and child development (0–16) in the home-based setting

Unit 3 The childcare practitioner in the home-based setting

Unit 4 Working in partnership with parents in the home-based setting

Unit 5 Meeting children's individual learning needs in the home-based setting.

In addition to this Diploma, CACHE are also offering a Level 2 qualification which will be called the Award/Certificate in Approved Child Carers (subject to QCA approval).

For more information about these new qualifications contact CACHE on 01727 847636 or look at their website www.cache.org.uk

NATIONAL VOCATIONAL QUALIFICATIONS FOR CHILDMINDERS (NVQ)

Some childminders choose to study for their National Vocational Qualification Level 3 in Children's Care, Learning and Development. NVQs are nationally recognised qualifications and students who have got to this level will already have gained valuable knowledge and understanding about childcare and all it entails. As childminders usually work alone, and therefore plan and organise their own work without any supervision, they should be studying at a level 3. Although it is not strictly necessary for childminders to have completed the CCP before enrolling on the NVQ level 3, I would definitely advise this course of action as the CCP provides the underpinning knowledge required for the NVQ level 3.

An NVQ is based on your actual working practice and it is necessary for your work to be assessed.

QUALITY ASSURANCE

Childminders can continue to develop and build on their training throughout their careers and Quality Assurance is a way of showing prospective and existing customers that you are committed to your business and that you are a *professional* childminder.

Quality Assurance schemes help childminders to be 'reflective practitioners' and encourage them to think about their practice; the way they do things and ultimately how improvements can be made. The government, and indeed the parents of the children you will look after, are demanding higher standards of childcare and it is your duty to ensure that you provide the highest possible standard of care. Quality Assurance is a way of proving that your service has been checked and that it is of a high standard.

CHILDMINDING NETWORKS

Childminding networks are run by many different organisations including local authorities and the National Childminding Association. As a registered childminder you may have the opportunity to become involved in a childminding network and the services and support they offer are useful. Childminders who are part of a network will receive regular visits from a coordinator who will assist with training, support meetings, loan schemes etc.

COMMUNITY CHILDMINDING

It is possible for some childminders to become involved in community childminding networks. These networks are set up in order to arrange care for children who have been referred by social services. They may offer respite care or perhaps temporary full-time care for families who are experiencing difficulties. Childminders who are involved in community networks will receive extra training aimed at caring for children in need, or from vulnerable or distressed backgrounds.

ACCREDITED CHILDMINDERS AND EARLY YEARS EDUCATION

It is possible for network childminders to take extra training to become accredited. This enables them to offer early years education for three and four year olds.

All three and four-year-old children in England are now able to receive five free nursery education sessions per week, if their parents wish. At present the free nursery entitlement is 12½ hours per week. By becoming accredited, childminders are able to claim government funding for offering this service to families. Childminders who are accredited on the National Childminding Association's Children Come First approved networks are, at present, the only childminders able to offer early years education sessions.

Accredited childminders, along with all other early years education settings such as nurseries and pre-schools, must be inspected by Ofsted if in England and the National Care Standards Inspectorate (CSIW) if in Wales and agree to follow a set curriculum.

FURTHER TRAINING OPPORTUNITIES

In addition to the recognised qualifications it is possible for childminders to access a variety of other training courses including seminars, conferences and workshops. It is a good idea for childminders to assess which areas you feel you need extra training in; and contact your local authority with regard to the availability of workshops or conferences which cover these topics.

Local authorities often run extra training in areas such as equal opportunities, managing children's behaviour, record keeping and food hygiene to name but a few. Additional training for child protection is also available and I would strongly advise all childminders to consider taking up this training. Your local authority can advise you about available courses and a short, distance learning programme, run through the National Society for the Prevention of Cruelty to Children (NSPCC) and Educare, is also available. Child Protection Awareness Programmes highlight the basics needed to understand, recognise and report on acts of child abuse. For details of these programmes and others which you may find useful you can contact NSPCC Educare on their programme hotline 01926 436219.

◆ TIP ◆

Training is a vital part of your job and it is necessary that you keep up to date on all aspects of childcare.

Finally, it is important for childminders to recognise the need for on-going training. To provide a professional service you need to be aware of any changes in procedures and legislation and never allow your training to become stale. The more skills you acquire, the better your childminding service will be, and you should always be looking for ways to improve and add to the knowledge you already have.

14

The National Childminding Association

THE ROLE OF THE NATIONAL CHILDMINDING ASSOCIATION

The National Childminding Association was set up in 1977 by childminders, parents and local authority workers. The Association is a unique charity and membership organisation which helps and supports childminders.

The NCMA works closely with the government and Welsh Assembly and provides a voice for childminders and home-based child carers, ensuring that our views and opinions are heard. Legislation which affects childminding, is monitored by the NCMA and any relevant information is passed on to its members.

The National Childminding Association works hard to promote childminding in a variety of different ways such as:

- campaigning on issues which NCMA members feel strongly about;

- developing specialist training and Quality Assurance schemes;

- supporting and encouraging childminding groups;

- producing and selling products which have been designed specifically for childminders, including contracts, record and accident books;

- offering public liability insurance and legal representation specifically tailored to childminders' needs.

During my years working as a childminder I have been a member of the National Childminding Association and I would thoroughly recommend that all new childminders consider joining the Association. The NCMA offers a variety of subscription packages to suit both individual and group childminders and you should contact them for further details.

THE BENEFITS OF NCMA MEMBERSHIP

Special deals for members

You will benefit from certain special offers and discounted rates which have been negotiated by the NCMA on products such as:

- **Healthcare** cash plan covering such things as dental and optical fees.
- **Breakdown services.**
- **Unsecured loans** from £2,000 to £25,000.
- **Toy** store discount of 10 per cent off purchases in store.

You will also receive copies of the membership magazine *Who Minds?*. The magazine is sent out four times per year and is packed with useful up-to-date information on government policies, health and safety, days out, childminding news, special offers, readers' letters etc.

Products

You will be entitled to purchase any of the products they supply at a discounted rate. The NCMA has developed tools which are invaluable to the smooth running of a childminding business such as:

- Inland Revenue-approved cash books;
- accident books;
- medical records;
- receipt books;
- advertising packages;
- training aids;
- childminding journals;
- aprons, tabards, bags, badges, fleeces etc bearing the NCMA logo.

Services

You will also be entitled to services such as:

- **NCMA Information Line**: This is a free information helpline for childminders, offering advice on all aspects of childminding including pay and conditions, contracts, allegations of child abuse etc. It can be a very worthwhile service for childminders, particularly those new to the profession or for those coming across a problem they have not encountered before. Impartial, confidential advice is invaluable.

- **Legal Advice Line**: Another free helpline, this time offering professional advice on legal problems such as contracts and pay disputes.

◆ TIP ◆

If you decide to become a member of the National Childminding Association you can sign up for a suitable membership package by contacting the NCMA on 020 8290 8999 or visiting their website at www.ncma.org.uk.

Useful Contacts

Care Standards Inspectorate for Wales (CSIW), National Assembly for Wales, Cardiff Bay, Cardiff CF99 1NA. Tel: 029 20 825111. Website: www.csiw.wales.gov.uk

Council for Awards in Children's Care and Education (CACHE), Beaufort House, Grosvenor Road, St Albans, Hertfordshire AL1 3AW. Tel: 01727 818616. Website: www.cache.org.uk. Email: info@cache.org.uk

Department for Education and Skills (DfES). Tel: 0870 000 2288. Website: www.dfes.gov.uk. Email: info@dfes.gov.uk

Equal Opportunities Commission, Arndale House, Arndale Centre, Manchester M4 3EQ. Tel: 0845 601 5901. Website: www.eoc.org.uk. Email: info@eoc.org.uk

Inland Revenue. Tel: 0845 300 3900 (helpline for Working Families Tax Credit). Website: www.inlandrevenue.gov.uk

Kidscape, 2 Grosvenor Gardens, London SW1W 0DH. Tel: 020 7730 3300 or helpline: 08451 205 204. Website: www.kidscape.org.uk

National Association for Toy and Leisure Libraries, 68 Churchway, London NW1 1LT. Tel: 020 7255 4600. Website: www.natll.org.uk Email: admin@playmatters.co.uk

National Care Standards Inspectorate (Wales) CSIW. Tel: 01443 848 450. Website: www.wales.gov.uk/subisocialpolicycarestandards/index.htm

National Childminding Association, 81 Tweedy Road, Bromley, Kent BR1 1TW. Tel: 0845 880 0044. Website: www.ncma.org.uk. Email: info@ncma.org.uk

National Extension College. The Michael Young Centre, Purbeck Road, Cambridge CB2 2HN. Tel: 0800 389 2839. Website: www.nec.ac.uk/courses

National Society for the Prevention of Cruelty to Children (NSPCC), Weston House, 42 Curtain Road, London EC2A 3NH. Tel: 020 7825 2500 or helpline: 0808 800 5000. Website: www.nspcc.org.uk

Northern Ireland Childminding Association (NICMA). Tel: 028 90 52059. Website: www.nicma.org

Office for Standards in Education (Ofsted), Alexandra House, 33 Kingsway, London WC2B 6SE. Tel: 020 7421 6800.
Website: www.ofsted.gov.uk

Royal Society for the Prevention of Accidents (RoSPA), Edgbaston Park, 353 Bristol Road, Edgbaston, Birmingham B5 7ST. Tel: 0121 248 2000. Website: www.rospa.com. Email: help@rospa.co.uk

Scottish Childminding Association, Suite 3, 7 Melville Terrace, Stirling FK8 2ND. Tel: 01786 445377.
Website: www.childminding.org

Scottish Commission for the Regulation of Care, Compass House, Discovery Quay, 11 Riverside Drive, Dundee DD1 4NY. Tel: 01382 207 100/0845 60 30890. Website: www.carecommission.com

Index

abuse
  allegations against childminders,
    30–1, 141, 143, 174
  protection from allegations, 141–3
  recognising, 30
  signs of abuse, 30, 136–40
  support following allegations, 143
  training, 168, 171
  types of abuse, 136–40
accidents
  prevention indoors, 17–18, 42–8
  prevention outdoors, 17–18, 48–50
  records of, 23, 141
  risk assessment, 19–23, 43–50
accidents and emergencies, 57–9, 67
accounts, 68, 95–108
accredited childminders, 17, 171
advertising, 69–72, 98, 108, 174
anti-discriminatory practice, 25, 120,
  123
Area Child Protection Committee
  (ACPC), 29–30, 140
assertiveness, 63, 72
assessment of children, 126–8
assistants, 13–15, 35, 66–9, 107

babies, 5–6, 9, 31–2, 55–6, 62, 75, 81,
  111, 125, 168
behaviour
  inappropriate, 138, 142
  managing unwanted, 27–8, 119–22,
    159, 168
  smacking, 27
books, 6, 45, 134
business matters
  accounts, 68, 95–108
  contracts, 62–3, 74–5, 78–94, 108,

    120, 146, 149–52, 159, 175
  filling vacancies, 5, 10, 69–72, 78,
    105, 108, 129
  insurance, 9, 21, 53, 64, 68, 79, 98,
    105, 107, 173
  milk refunds, 9–10, 98, 102
  tax and national insurance, 95–6
    102–3

care, learning and play, 16–17, 132–5,
  158
Certificate in Childminding Practice
  (CCP), 71, 167–8
checks,
  equipment, 19, 124–5
  toys, 19, 124–5
childminders, working with 2, 66–9
child protection, 30, 36, 136–43, 159–
  60
child:staff ratios, 14–16, 67, 157
Children's Information Service
  (CIS), 7, 70
comfort objects, 76, 138
community childminding, 170
complaints, 28–9, 144–54
confidentiality, 29, 31, 118, 120, 122–
  3, 142–3, 147, 150, 153
contracts
  disputes, 150
  negotiating, 78–94
  reasons for, 151–2
  reviewing, 93–4
  signing, 92–3
  terminating, 94
Council for Awards in Children's
  Care and Education (CACHE),
  167–8

council tax, 100–1
Criminal Records Bureau (CRB), 36–7

deposits, 85
Developing Childminding Practice
(DCP), 167–8
development, 17–18, 126–7
diaries, 118–19
diet, 24–5, 110–11, 116–17, 159
special, 24, 81–2, 159
difficult
people, 145, 148–50
situations, 145–6
discrimination, 25–6, 120, 123
disputes, contract, 150–1
documentation, 30-1, 160

Early Learning Goals, 17
Early Years Development and
Childcare Partnership (EYDCP),
9–10, 130
emergencies, 57–9, 67
emotional abuse, 138–9
enforcement, Ofsted, 12, 162
equal opportunities, 25–6, 120, 123
equipment, 5–8, 18–19, 51–3, 158
exercise, 17–18, 135
expenses, 78–82, 98–102
Extending Childminding Practice
(ECP), 167–8
extras, 80–2
evacuation procedures, 126

family
effects on, 2–3
fees, setting, 78–80
fire drills, 126
first aid, 58–9, 166–7
first meeting, 73–4
financial help, 8–10
food and drink, 24–5, 110–11, 116–17, 159

gardens, 48–50
grading Ofsted, 155–6
grants
start–up, 9

sustainability, 10
groups
playgroup, 89–90
support, 128–9

health, 21–4, 55–7, 158–9
health visitors, 130
heat and light, 100–01
holidays
bank, 61, 86–7
childminder, 85
parent, 85–6
home
effects of childminding on, 2–3
hygiene, 21–3, 55–7

illness, 87–8
inspections, 155–65
insurance
car, 53, 95
house, 95
public liability, 95
interviewing, potential customers,
72-3
Introducing Childminding Practice
(ICP), 166–7
investigation – Ofsted, 12

Kidscape, 143

late collections, 82, 145–6
losses business, 105–8

maternity leave, 90–1, 106–7
meals, 24–5, 110–11, 116–17, 159
menus, 117
milk refunds, 9–10, 98, 102

National Care Standards Inspectorate
(Wales) (CSIW), 170
National Childminding Association
(NCMA), 167, 172–4
National Society for the Prevention
of Cruelty to Children (NSPCC),
143, 172
National Standards, 13–31, 156–60
National Vocational Qualifications
(NVQs), 169

neglect, 137
nettles, 50
networks, 129
nurseries, 4, 89–90

observations, 126–8
Ofsted – aims of, 11
outdoor play, 135

parental permission, 124
passwords, 29
pets, 55, 57
physical abuse, 137–8
physical environment, 17–18, 158
planning, 109
play – types of, 132–5
playgroup, 89–90
poisoning
    intentional, 137
    plants, 49–50
policies
    maintain, 119–24
    write, 121–3
portfolios, 63–5, 73
premises, 17–18, 41–50, 73, 158
professionalism, 60, 73, 109, 144,
    147, 151
profit and loss, 103–8
punishment, 119–21

Quality Assurance, 170

rashes, 50
registration, 11–12
retainer fees, 83–4
routines
    babies and toddlers, 110–11
    schools, 111–13

Royal Society for the Prevention of
    Accidents, (RoSPA), 41

safety
    checklists for hazards, 43–50
    first aid, 58–9, 166–7
    hygiene, 21–3, 55–7
scalds and burns, 59
school
    homework, 112
    school runs, 8, 109–11
self-assessment, 163, 165
settling children, 75–6, 83
sexual abuse, 138
smacking, 27
snacks, 24–5, 110–11, 116–17, 159
special needs, 26–7, 159
suitable person, 13–14, 157
support for childminders, 143, 173

tax, 95–6, 102–3
tick charts, 128
toy libraries, 7
toys, 5–8, 51
training for childminders
    compulsory, 166–7
    courses, 166-71
    NVQs, 169

vacancies
    advertising, 69–72
    filling, 72–4
videos, 124, 128

wages, 68,
water rates, 100–1
wear and tear, 100–1
welcome pack, 65

Printed in Germany
by Amazon Distribution
GmbH, Leipzig